An Everlasting Covenant

Selected Sermons by
Rabbi Elliot J. Cosgrove

An Everlasting Covenant

Selected Sermons by
Rabbi Elliot J. Cosgrove

2009–2010 / 5770

An Everlasting Covenant: Selected Sermons by Rabbi Elliot J. Cosgrove
2009–2010 / 5770

Copyright ©2010 Park Avenue Synagogue

All rights reserved. No part of this publication may be reproduced, stored in a retrieval system, or transmitted, in any form or by any means, electronic, mechanical, photocopying, recording or otherwise, without prior permission.

ISBN 978-0-9825084-1-1

Printed in the United States of America in 2010

Park Avenue Synagogue
50 East 87th Street
New York, NY 10128
www.pasyn.org

Cover: The domed stained glass ceiling of Park Avenue Synagogue, designed by architect Walter Schneider in 1926 and dedicated in March 1927.
Photo: Malcolm Varon

Contents

Foreword	ix
Acknowledgments	xi
Preface	xii
Erev Rosh Hashanah *"The Journey Home"*	1
Rosh Hashanah *"People of Destiny"*	6
Shabbat Shuvah *"The Importance of Apologies"*	14
Yom Kippur *"Do you still love me?"*	20
Sukkot *"Judaism: Universal or Particular?"*	28
Noaḥ *"Two-by-Two"*	33
Toldot *"Judaism: Liberal or Conservative?"*	39
Va-yetzei *"Jewish and American"*	44

Va-yishlaḥ
  "Wars of Necessity, Wars of Choice" ... 49

Va-yeishev
  "The Joseph Generation" ... 54

B' shallaḥ
  "The Right to Be Different" ... 60

Yitro
  "Remembrance of Torah Past" ... 65

T'rumah
  "Esther, Vashti, and Other Uncomfortable Options
  for Jewish Women" ... 70

Va-yak·hel/P'kudei
  "Tradition and Change" ... 75

Va-yikra
  "Prisoner of Hope: 60th Yahrzeit of
  Rabbi Milton Steinberg, z"l" ... 81

Sunday, March 21, 2010
  Book Launch: Rabbi Milton Steinberg's
  The Prophet's Wife ... 86

Passover, First Day
  "Staying Power" ... 90

Passover, Eighth Day
  "The Four Children… of Grief and Recovery" ... 94

Aḥarei Mot/Kedoshim
  "Steamships and Start-ups" ... 99

Emor
  "Pesaḥ Sheni: *Second Chances*" ... 104

B'har/B'hukkotai
 "A Narrow Bridge" 109

B'midbar
 "Kugel on a Hot Sommer Day" 114

Shavuot, Second Day
 "Yizkor: Retrieving the Past" 119

Beha'alotkha
 *"What's So Funny About Boycott,
 Divestment, and Sanctions?"* 124

Korah
 "Pyramids of Success" 130

Park Avenue Synagogue 135

Park Avenue Synagogue Board of Trustees,
 Clergy, and Staff 137

Foreword

Listening to Rabbi Cosgrove's sermons on Shabbat and Festivals in our majestic sanctuary is a distinct privilege for all Park Avenue Synagogue congregants. His sermons during his second year as our Rabbi and teacher continue to reflect unparalleled scholarship, new insights into Torah, and meaning for the entire community.

Whether it was Rabbi Cosgrove's intention or not, it appears to me that there was a consistent theme in his messages, relating to "Community." He raised issues of Jewish continuity at Park Avenue Synagogue and in society at large, advised us about relationships within families and with friends, examined how our community opens its doors to singles and young families, considered how we educate students of all ages, and asked whether our Synagogue is meeting the needs of all its members.

His sermons raised as many thoughtful questions as they provided answers, ranging from how people want to be remembered and when people should give others a second chance, to questioning our practice of social justice.

In the video made for the Gala this past spring, Rabbi Cosgrove expressed his vision for the Park Avenue Synagogue community, saying that we aspire to be a community in which members and visitors are welcomed with warmth when they enter and noticed when they are absent.

In his final sermon of the year, related to Parashat Koraḥ, Rabbi Cosgrove wrote about the measurement and meaning of success and failure. This sermon sets the tone for his Rabbinate and reveals how dedicated Rabbi Cosgrove is to this community, to the larger Jewish community, and to Israel:

> "I, like many in this room, have experienced a few setbacks and thankfully enjoyed much for which I am deeply grateful. And I have come to know, as we all do, that there are times when we are recipients of misplaced criticism and times when we are granted undeserving praise. Which is why I am grateful for John Wooden's definition of success. Only I know if I gave it my all, only I know if I was true to my ideals, only I know if I did everything to become the best that I am capable of becoming."

I hope each reader of this book treasures Rabbi Cosgrove's words as I do, appreciates him, and is inspired by this leader who gives everything he has to make the Park Avenue Synagogue community the best it can be.

Steven M. Friedman, Chairman

Acknowledgments

This book would not be possible without the tireless and thoughtful efforts of Jean Bloch Rosensaft, Marga Hirsch, and Joanne Zablud. Their dedication to the Park Avenue Synagogue community is much appreciated.

Preface

"What do you think the Rabbi will speak about tomorrow?" When I was growing up, my father posed this question to his children every week at the Shabbat dinner table. Each member of the family would weigh in, trying to predict the topic of the next day's sermon. Would the Rabbi speak about Israel? A political issue? Or focus on an aspect of the Torah portion? The reward for guessing correctly was priceless. Two minutes into the Rabbi's sermon, the winning sibling would receive a wink and smile from everyone, the champion of the sermon pool – at least until the following Shabbat.

Years later, having grown up to become the rabbi writing the sermons, I can reflect more thoughtfully on how a sermon topic is chosen.

Imagine a triangle. At the corners stand the three poles that shape any sermon.

The first corner of the triangle is the Torah reading or the context of the Jewish calendar. A Rabbi is no mere motivational speaker. He or she has a responsibility to draw congregants closer to our sacred tradition. Any sermon preached from a synagogue pulpit must have a connection, no matter how slim, to either the scriptural reading or the synagogue year. It is a Rabbi's duty to make sure that every Jew present emerges from the synagogue that day feeling part of the grand narrative of our people.

The second corner shaping a sermon is what is on my mind. Sermons are forms of religious reflection and testimony, perhaps the most personal expression of my rabbinate and my vision of Jewish life. Writing a sermon is one of the few aspects of working in a synagogue that does not require a committee, a staff meeting, or a budget process. Sermons are opportunities to give voice to my concerns – personal, communal, or global – and to share my hopes and my love of Torah with my community.

The third and final corner is what is on *your* mind – the mind of the listener. No matter what the Torah reading, no matter what is pressing on my mind, a sermon is a genre of expression that occurs in the context of community. A sermon should be deeply relevant to the life of the listener. The best feeling I can elicit in a listener is the unnerving sensation that "I felt the Rabbi was speaking directly to me and my concerns." The concerns may be Jewish, secular or personal. Every week, before I sit down to write, I read the paper, speak to congregants, and consider what it is my community wants or needs to hear.

These three corners represent the three forces that shape my sermons. Any single sermon may favor one corner or another. Granted the opportunity to preach with some frequency, the promise of the following week's sermon eases my anxiety at having unduly favored one corner or another. A sermon that cannot be positioned somewhere within the above triangle is not, in my mind, a successful sermon. A great sermon is a sermon in which the three corners converge into a single point – anchored in Torah, deeply personal, and altogether relevant to the congregant. The present volume represents my efforts towards achieving this goal last year.

I am grateful to our Chairman, Steven M. Friedman, for his friendship, encouragement, and mentorship. Our dialogue and partnership far exceed my highest hopes of what a lay-clergy relationship can be. I thank the Officers and Board of Park Avenue Synagogue for their ongoing support and enthusiastic efforts towards bringing our congregation to its fullest potential. As the "not so new" rabbi, I can express deep thanks to the entire community for the friendships formed over the past two years. I suppose as you come to know me better, you will be able to predict with greater accuracy what my sermon will be about each coming Shabbat. This also means, of course, that I have gotten to know *you* better, and am better able to speak to your hearts and minds. These clergy-congregant relationships, forged daily, are sacred building blocks for creating the community of our dreams. I look forward to the years ahead.

Thank you so much to Jean Bloch Rosensaft for directing the publication of the book. Your kindness, expertise, leadership, and volunteer spirit exemplify the very best of our community. I especially want to thank my wonderful colleagues Marga Hirsch and Joanne Zablud for their painstaking efforts towards making this volume possible.

I dedicate this book to the very individuals with whom I began – my siblings – Ben, Danny, and Jason Cosgrove (and their families). Born of the same DNA and raised at the same Shabbat table, I am grateful for your ongoing willingness to share your thoughts, insights and humor towards helping me generate sermons. I treasure our exchanges as a means towards crafting a message, and more importantly, as a way to build our friendships into the years ahead. In this spirit, I also include my wife's siblings – Andrea, Jeff, and Nancy (and their families) – whose friendship and input I also prize. Siblings are perhaps both the most important and least examined of our familial relationships. We should dedicate much more than books to them.

L'ma'an aḥai v'rei'ai adabra na shalom bakh. For my brothers and friends I say: "Peace be within thee." (Psalm 122:7)

Erev Rosh Hashanah
"The Journey Home"

This year marks the 150th anniversary of the birth of Sholom Aleichem. Russian-born, settling in America in 1914, Aleichem has been called the "natural genius of Yiddish Literature." (Irving Howe, *A Treasury of Yiddish Stories*, p. 74) If you have ever read a Sholom Aleichem story, then you know that the appeal of his prodigious literary legacy is in his ability to package evocative and complex themes in seemingly innocent anecdotes and tales.

This evening, I want to share with you one of his most famous stories, called "On Account of a Hat." It is based on a well-known joke. It is a tale about coming home for the holidays, a comedy of errors, sort of a *Trains, Planes, and Automobiles* meets *shtetl* life. The main action takes place in a train station. Sholem Shachnah, our *schlemiel* protagonist, clinches a real estate deal and is rushing to go home for the holidays. After days of travel, he arrives at the Zlodievke train station, exhausted, with one more train to go. Fearful that he will fall asleep and miss the train, he tips the porter to wake him up when it arrives. He sits down in the train station next to a slumbering Gentile official, perhaps an inspector or maybe even a provincial commander. The official's high status is signaled by the military hat with a red band and a visor nestled over his sleeping head. The train arrives in the middle of the night. When the porter wakes Sholem up from his deep sleep, Sholem, in a daze, mistakenly grabs the sleeping official's hat. He gets on the train, and finds himself treated with unusual deference and respect by the ticket agent, the conductor, and everyone else. He is advised not to sit in third class with the riffraff, nor in second, but "His Excellency" has a seat waiting in first class.

Sholem is confused and frustrated, believing himself to be the object of mockery. He then glances at a mirror on the train to see the cause of all the fawning. Sitting atop Sholem's head is the official's hat with the visor and red band. What bad luck, he says to himself, I told the porter to wake me up, but what does he do, he wakes up the official instead, which means... that I must still be asleep on the bench. At which point, our hero scoops up his belongings and runs back to the bench in the station where he was sleeping. Thus, recounts our narrator, Sholem misses the train as it leaves the station and, as a result, misses the entire holiday.

It is an odd tale, a bit comic, a bit enigmatic, a tad tragic. It has been analyzed time and again by literary theorists. A story about the vagaries of modern life, about Jewish-Gentile relations in the Pale of Settlement, a psychological parable about the identities society thrusts upon each of us.

This evening, I want to suggest to you that at its core, it is a tale about coming home – one Jew's desire to go home for the holidays and his inability to do so, because, as the punch line of the story makes clear, he thought he was the wrong person. The thrust of the tale seems to be that "identity" and "homecoming" are interdependent. We can come home, but only insofar as we know who we are. Conversely, and by extension, the trains that we miss, physically and spiritually, we miss because we forget or reject who we really are.

This evening begins Rosh Hashanah, our annual homecoming. We see new and familiar faces, new members and returning ones, some who were not here since the last holidays, some who were here as recently as today's morning *minyan*. All of us are returning, to the synagogue and to this sacred date on the Jewish calendar, Rosh Hashanah, our new year. The sounds, smells, tastes of *yontif* all beckon us. I welcome each of you and look forward to a holiday season and a year ahead filled with health, happiness, and prosperity for our families, for the Jewish people, and for all of humanity.

If there is one consistent thread and theme in our tradition, it is the idea of coming home. Think about it. Most of the Torah is a tale of how the Jewish people sought to return to the land first promised to Abraham. The trek to "The Promised Land" is a return home, not a journey to a new place. Thousands of years of Jewish history occurred in exile, filled with a longing for our home, as we sat by the rivers of Babylon, by rivers all around the world, longing to return. There is not a single Jewish service that does not contain within it an expressed desire to return. And it is not merely geography that is at stake, it is our fundamental posture of being as Jews, a desire to return. Long before Homer's tale of Odysseus' homeward voyage, in fact, ever since the expulsion of Adam and Eve from the Garden, our tradition teaches that authentic religious feeling is situated on the impulse to reclaim, to return to our roots. Every day this past month, as we will later this evening, Jews have chanted Psalm 27, for the Days of Awe. Embedded within is one request, our highest hope and deepest desire, to return to God's house. It is the supplication of a person seeking homecoming. Sholom Aleichem's story is quintessentially Jewish because it is a story about one man's attempts to arrive back home.

So tonight, let me turn the question to you by way of our Sholom Aleichem story. If "homecoming" and "identity" are intertwined, then for you, here this evening, where are you and to what are you returning? The very first recorded question of the Bible – "Where are you?" – is posed by God to Adam. God asks it, of course, for existential reasons, not geographical ones. It is the same question that is posed to us tonight. How far have you ventured from your roots in the past year? You may be here in this room, but how far from home do you remain? Each of us, I would like to think, possesses an internal compass, a sense of right and wrong, a list of priorities, a belief in who we are and what we aspire to be. But in the year that has passed, we have left our home far behind and find ourselves tourists to our own identities. Our lives have taken us far afield and we have found ourselves in spiritual exile. You may be in *shul* this evening, but you still need to ask, are you recognizable to those around you, to yourself, to your God?

So many relationships – in the workplace, in our community, in our families – are derailed from where they should be. Our disputes and disagreements are painful because we know the potential of how things should be, perhaps how things once were. It is actually not that hard to be in dispute with someone with whom we presume we could never get along. The sadness wrought by our quarrels has to do with our awareness of just how far things are from where they should be. The holidays are our yardage marker signaling just how distant we are from those we love – a friend to whom we no longer speak, an intractable grudge between parent and child. How did we allow that one misdeed to eclipse the totality of a relationship? Our vanity, our egos, conceit, and pride prevent us from softening our stance, from issuing apologies, and from accepting them from those extending them to us with sincerity.

A Hasidic parable tells of a king who, in a fit of rage against his son, exiled him from his kingdom. The son wandered alone through the world. In time, the king's heart softened, and he sent his ministers to find his son and ask him to return. They found the young prince, but he answered them saying he could not return to the kingdom, he had been too hurt and his heart still harbored bitterness. The ministers brought back the sad news to the king. The king told them to return to his son with the following message: "Return home as far as you can, and I will come the rest of the way." Tonight, we begin to journey home. Tonight the possibility for dialogue begins and we open up the crack of hope towards reconciliation.

Harder than the journey towards each other, is the second journey, the journey within, to arrive home to our true selves. Hermann Hesse once wrote "Each person ha[s] only one genuine vocation – to find the way to himself..." This evening we begin to acknowledge all those wrong turns that have resulted in each of us becoming alienated from who we really are; when we, like Jonah, knew the direction we were supposed to go, but decided to go the opposite way. Jews, unlike Christians, don't believe that our original condition is sinful. Our shortcomings, our failings, our sins – these are painful because they have resulted in us being separated from our potential. We engage in repentance, *teshuvah*, not out of fear of punishment or retaliation, we engage in *teshuvah* because each of us wants to return home, each of us yearns to be reconciled with the person we know we can be. Our homecoming, as Sholom Aleichem knew, is all about our ability to reconnect to our true selves.

Finally, our return, we know, is not merely to each other, or to ourselves, but to God. This is what the prophet of the holidays, Isaiah, meant when he wrote: "Your sins have separated you from your God." (Isa. 59:2) Our tradition teaches that within the human being dwells the soul that is a spark of God. In returning, we seek to find that piece of the Divine that desperately wants to be found. The promise of these Days of Awe is that God will accept us in all our faults as long as we are honest about who we really are. Neither the quantity nor the quality of our sins precludes us from being received back by our Creator. Tradition teaches that God's assurance to Israel is "Open unto me the door of repentance, be it even as narrow as the point of a needle, I will open it so wide that wagons and chariots can pass through." (Pesikta de Rav Kahana, 163b) The promise of the holidays is that, if you are willing, God will, under all circumstances, accept you.

Three journeys home. Towards each other, towards ourselves, and towards God. Each journey is difficult. None is possible without coming to terms with who we really are, where we fell short, and who we believe we can be.

There is a legend about a group of angels who, having heard that God intended to create the human being in God's own likeness, plotted to hide the Divine image. One angel proposed hiding it on the pinnacle of the highest mountain, but a wiser angel pointed out that the human is an ambitious climber and would ascend the highest peak. Another angel suggested that the Image be sunk beneath the deepest ocean. This angel too was dissuaded when another pointed out that the human is curious and would plumb the ocean depths and draw forth the hidden treasure. The shrewdest angel counseled that the Image should be hidden within the human being himself because it is the last place that he would be likely to look for it. Tonight, we embark on the most ambitious journey home of all: the attempt to re-discover our own soul, the Divine image, the key to unlocking the relationships that matter the most to us. Tonight, we begin our journey home.

Rosh Hashanah
"People of Destiny"

In his collection of stories on the High Holy Days, *Sippurei Yom Hakippurim*, Shai Agnon, the towering figure of modern Hebrew literature, makes repeated use of the symbol of the *tallit*. For Agnon it comes to represent much more than a mere piece of cloth. In one of the stories, *Pi Shnayim*, "Twice Over," the protagonist sits at home before the holidays unable to decide which of two *tallitot* to wear. Like some of us, he owns more than one. The first one he received as part of an inheritance. His father-in-law was a great scholar and had an extraordinary collection of *sefarim*, of holy books. When his father-in-law died, the books were divided up by the children. One special book that was sent to him was sent wrapped in a *tallit*. This *tallit* came to represent his past, the old world; the voices of his predecessors. The second *tallit* was very different; he had purchased this one for himself. When he made *aliyah* to Israel, he bought a new *tallit*. He had moved into a neighborhood full of Hasidim and whatever type of *tallit* they wore, he wanted to have the same kind and fit right in. This second *tallit* represented everything he hoped to be. It was his unrealized future.

So with the two *tallitot* before him, the story unfolds. Our man conducts an internal debate on which one he should wear to synagogue that holiday. The new one, the one that represents his future, symbolic of the life he so desperately wants, or the old one, the one that signifies his past, not only his father-in-law, but the learning and values of the old world, an almost mythical yesteryear that he sought to embrace. He agonizes, deliberates, sits in anguish, measuring the merits of each one and finally, unable to decide, he lays them both out, closes his eyes, and takes whichever one is closer and runs to *shul*. He arrives at *shul*, and walks in… to an empty sanctuary. Services are over. His deliberations caused him to miss the critical moment of prayer. His inability to decide between the two *tallitot* prevented him from arriving at all. Agnon writes: "There I was like an apothecary, so long at work mixing powders for a drug, that in the meantime the patient dies."

If you are sitting in this room, then you have made it further than the character in Agnon's story. Agnon's story gives voice to the truth that our lives, limited in length, contain a finite number of opportunities and, far too often, inertia and indecision at critical moments result in our undoing.

Today, Rosh Hashanah, is not merely about counting time from 5769 to 5770 but, as Agnon's story brings home, about making every opportunity count. The ancient Greeks actually had two words for time. The first word refers to the passage of time, the steady progress of minutes, hours, and days – *chronos*. The second kind of time, the moment of decision or opportunity, is called *kairos*. Today, on Rosh Hashanah we are alert to both kinds of time, a new year and new opportunities. Our tragedies are when we fall victim to Mark Twain's lament that "I was seldom able to see an opportunity until it had ceased to be one." Our joy, our aspirations, our heroism – all are found in our ability to be present and responsive to the challenges and opportunities of the moment.

History is filled with instances when we have been faced with a choice of how to respond at a critical juncture, to go one way or the other, to take action or to linger in our inertia. I think of over 100 years ago, when Russian Jewry faced persecution and pogroms and the first wave of immigration, *aliyah*, took place. A group called the BILU, an acronym for *Beit Yaakov L'khu V'nelkha*, "O House of Jacob, get up and go," were Jewish pioneers who transformed Jewish life by taking courageous steps towards the creation of a Jewish State in the Ottoman empire. I think of Theodore Herzl, who in the wake of the Dreyfus Affair, hatched the plan for a political State of Israel, boldly announcing, "If you will it, it is no dream."

Just over fifty years ago, when American Jewry was hemming and hawing over the modern State of Israel, the spokesman for Modern Orthodoxy, Rabbi Joseph Soloveitchik, employed the poetic imagery of the Song of Songs to speak to our people in one of his most famous addresses, called *"Kol Dodi Dofek*, The Voice of My Beloved Knocks." On Yom Ha'atzmaut 1956, just over a decade following the Holocaust and a few short years after the establishment of the State of Israel, he called Diaspora Jewry of his generation to task. Reeling from the physical and spiritual trauma of Auschwitz, Jews were numb to the theological and practical implications of a modern Jewish State. Soloveitchik compared us to a slumbering lover. While we slept, the voice of our beloved, our destiny, was knocking; we couldn't or wouldn't hear it and were missing the moment of opportunity. Soloveitchik's address, given in Hebrew, is often titled in English "Fate and Destiny." To be a people of fate, he explained, is to be a people who resign themselves to a condition, a set of circumstances, to be passive participants in the unfolding of chronological time. To be a people of destiny signifies a deliberate and conscious existence, a people that has chosen to chart out its own destiny and seize its moment.

So where are we today? As a Jewish people, as a community, gathering together on Rosh Hashanah, we need to ask: when someone looks back to characterize our historical moment, what will they say? By all accounts, our age is a decisive one, for us as Jews, as Americans, and as members of a common humanity. There is a palpable caution in the air, as we sit nervously weighing the options before us. Whatever the issue is, no matter what your politics may be, one can sense it. Health care, the economy, the wars that we fight – we are unsure as to which foot to put forward. Israel faces mounting threats from Iran and increasing criticism in the world court, where even her most liberal supporters are hard pressed to see peace with neighbors who refuse to recognize her right to exist. Our core institutions like JTS and UJA face generational challenges. Our apprehensions, of course, are deeply personal. In the year gone by, I have sat with many members of our community, deeply bruised by the loss of a job, the loss of security. Many of us are searching for a path forward. Like the figure in Agnon's story, we know we have to take our next step, but we are not sure quite how – and in our indecision, we risk missing the moment.

Today, fifty years after Soloveitchik's speech, a hundred years after Herzl, I believe we are in the midst of a moment of destiny. Long after our lives have ended, I think people will look back at this juncture in history and ask whether we missed our moment. I believe this not because America and Israel have never faced challenges before, not because our anxieties are of a different quality or quantity than ever before. I believe that our moment is a decisive one, a moment of destiny, because I am a Jew. To be Jewish in 2009, 1959, 1909 or any other time, means that you lead your life, each day, believing that it is a moment of destiny, that the demands of today are insistent and particular and pressing in a way they weren't yesterday and won't be tomorrow. Heschel wrote that "Every age, every epoch constitutes a turning point." To be Jewish means to be part of a nervous, unsettling, and angst-ridden condition that also inspires, motivates, and stirs us to activity at every age.

Many of you may remember the bestselling book *Passages*, by Gail Sheehy. It came out in the 1970s, making it a bit before my time, but then again, when you are a Rabbi, nearly every book you read is "before your time." From what I understand, the book caused quite a stir because it was the first popular psychology book to map out the developmental stages of adult life. Sheehy claimed, and I think this is now widely accepted, that it is not just children who go through emotional and intellectual maturation, but adults as well. Each passage, whether it is during your 20's, 40's, 60's or 80's is inevitable. Some of these passages are marked by events that are natural and joyous, such as going away to college, getting married, having children, or getting a job. Others are unexpected and often sad, such as losing a job, divorce, the untimely death of a loved one. But no matter what the event or developmental stage, each passage leaves a person exposed and vulnerable. Each passage, joyous or tragic, brings with it a degree of pain as we leave the familiarity of one stage for the uncertainty of the next. Yet by allowing ourselves to be exposed and vulnerable, we are also yeasty and embryonic again, capable of stretching in ways we hadn't known before. These passages are inevitable and it is not within our power to pretend they are not there. What is in our control, however, Sheehy tells us, is our response: whether we choose to view a passage as an opportunity for change, to renew and redefine ourselves, to recreate both ourselves and the conditions in which we live. "Life," wrote the poet Friedrich Hebbel, "is not anything; it is only the opportunity for something." Who we are – as a people, as a nation, as an institution – is a function of our ability to move with deliberate intention, in Hebrew, *kavannah*, through life's transformative moments.

Last year, on Rosh Hashanah I announced my intention to see the Park Avenue Synagogue community through fresh eyes, to experience it "as is," and to learn its melody before I sing my own. It has been an exciting year and I am grateful for all the kindness extended to me, to Debbie, and to my family as we have settled in, and for the patience you have shown as I have begun to learn the rhythms of our synagogue. Every single day, I am humbled by the deep and textured commitments made to this synagogue; every single day, I am thankful to my predecessors for having built the institution now entrusted to my care.

This moment, our moment, my moment, must be a moment of destiny for our synagogue. We dare not be passive participants as tectonic shifts take place. We must leverage the challenges facing us, Israel, and humanity and create the right institutional response. We will not resign ourselves to fate. It is simply unacceptable to say that "I was bored in Hebrew School so my children will be as well." We will create anew and challenge the models in place. It is inconceivable to me to conduct a Shabbat Service that does not speak to the hearts and minds of those hundreds of members we seek to serve. You may come or not, but we must aspire towards a prayer experience that serves the needs of your Jewish soul and the souls of those who have yet to walk into this building. We cannot act surprised by the decision of our grown children not to enter the synagogue of their youth when we ourselves are not doing outreach to unaffiliated twenty- and thirty-somethings. How can we grumble about tepid support for Israel, the future of Conservative Judaism, and a decreasing investment in the social service agencies of New York City and national Jewish life, as if we ourselves are not stakeholders invested in the outcome?

If you are concerned about Israel's future, then you can begin to show that concern by joining me and thousands of other Americans as we protest the president of Iran's visit to the U.N. this Thursday at noon. I didn't choose to live at this moment of history, but I do, and so do you, and it is my intention to leave Israel, my Judaism, the Judaism of my children, and the Judaism of the community I have been charged to lead in better shape than it would be without me. It makes no sense to me to wax nostalgic about Jewish life as if it were a fairy tale, with stories of our parents' *seder* tables and grandparents' love of Israel. Shouldn't we strive for a Jewish life today as good as yesterday? Shouldn't tomorrow be even better?

Charles Dickens began *David Copperfield* by announcing: "Whether I shall turn out to be the hero of my own life, or whether that station will be held by anybody else, these pages must show." Today, on Rosh Hashanah, there's a new book, and we're going to write it. Too often we say to ourselves, I'll change some other time. Right now is not the best time for me, I can't commit to anything at the moment. When things are different, when I can manage, when the weather changes, when I get some help, when the children go to school, when they come back for the holidays. Right now, as we stand on the precipice of a new year, we dare not say "when we get to it." We know that every moment counts. It is now that we must take action, not later.

Today is a day to begin anew, to make a change in essence, a redirection of the inner person. Habit and conditioning often combine to keep a person torn between inertia and the desire for improvement. We are like the man in the old story, stuck in a prison for many years, simply because he never realized that the door to his cell was never locked.

Against all the forces which proclaim that we cannot change, the High Holy Days teach that we have the capacity for change. It is not a choice between optimism or pessimism. It is about putting one foot in front of the other. Speaking at a moment of crisis in the 1920s, one of the greatest preachers of the twentieth century, Rabbi Israel Levinthal, explained that we are all given the choice of how we pilot the ships of our lives. We can drift, he said, or we can steer. We can surrender to the elements, or we can move deliberately and with intention towards our hoped-for destination.

In this room, right now, there are men and women, sitting with the difficult choices, the *tallitot* of life before them, wanting to understand how to move forward in what appears to be intractable situations. A father and son, unable to reconcile after a hurt long in the past, but still eclipsing the present. A young couple, stuck for far too long in a status quo, unable to take the brave step forward to commitment. A retiree seeking to reconstitute himself in a new chapter of life. A spouse mourning the loss of a life partner, unable to find a path forward. These are not made-up stories, these are your stories and there are so many more, at least as many as the beating hearts in this room.

For the last several years, every summer I find myself teaching another one of my children how to ride a bike. I have come to realize that the most difficult part of learning to ride a bike isn't balance – once they are moving, kids pretty much get it. The trickiest part isn't stopping; they figure that out along the way, sometimes the hard way, but they figure it out. The hardest part isn't turning; that actually comes rather naturally. The toughest part for a child about riding a bike is starting, going from a complete standstill and pressing forward.

The High Holy Days are intended to give us the courage to start up again, even when we have stumbled and fallen. My favorite *midrash* associated with today is about God's creation of the world. The *midrash* tells us that before God created this world, the one in which we all live, God had in fact created many worlds, but was unhappy with each of them. Only after several failed attempts did God finally arrive at our current configuration. Think about it for a second, this is God we are talking about, God doesn't make mistakes, yet this *midrash* tells us that even God had to have that painful realization, that moment of reflection, necessary to leave one world behind and create a new one.

Today is Rosh Hashanah, a day when we ask ourselves to be creators of worlds. We look at the world in which we have lived and ask if it is the one which we want for next year. As Martin Buber wrote "In the man who does *teshuvah*, creation begins anew; in his renewal the substance of the world is renewed." (*On Judaism*, p. 67) For some of us, the task is to create an entirely new world because the current one is no longer working. For others, it will simply be to approach the same world with renewed and creative energy. Either way, we must find the courage which God found, to draw on the right mixture of faith, self-reliance, and resilience to push forward to become the families and individuals we so desperately want to be. Each of us must take new steps in the days before Yom Kippur, commit to creating new worlds, to letting go of a past stage with its satisfactions and failures, all in order to find the richness of the next.

There is a story in the Talmud about a man named Eliezer ben Durdaya. He came from a fine background and a great future was predicted for him. However, he strayed from the righteous path and his life was derailed by his own shortcomings. One day he heard a voice from heaven tell him "Eliezer ben Durdaya, you have no share in the world to come." He was moved to repentance and he cried out "*Harim bikshu alai raḥamim*, O ye mountains, plead for me." When they refused, he said, "*Shemesh v'yareaḥ*, sun and moon, plead for me." They also turned him down. He then said, "*Kokhavim u-mazalot*, stars and planets, plead for me," and they too refused. Finally, Eliezer sat down and, after much soul searching, he melted in tears and said, "*Ein ha-davar talu elah bi*, it depends on nothing except me." With that, a voice from heaven proclaimed, "*M'zuman hu l'ḥayei olam ha-ba*, he is now ready to take his place in the world to come."

Rosh Hashanah is our bridge to tomorrow. The tools to get there are here, in this community, in our families, within each and every one of us. Let us reach within and grow, step by step, with intention, and together we will arrive at our destiny.

Shabbat Shuvah
"The Importance of Apologies"

Sincere apologies, it would seem, are our nation's fastest diminishing resource. A few weeks ago, many of you may have watched one of the oddest and perhaps most unsatisfying endings to a U.S. Open tennis match, as Serena Williams strenuously and rather inelegantly objected to the linesman's call of a foot fault violation. For her unsportsmanlike conduct she was penalized the point, which was match point, thus losing the match, and additionally fined more than ten thousand dollars.

More disappointing than the outburst, which, given illustrious predecessors like John "You've got to be kidding me" McEnroe, was not in itself unprecedented, was her subsequent non-apology apology. This was her statement:

> Everyone could see the passion I have for my job. Now that I have had time to regain my composure, I can see that, while I do not agree with the line call, in the heat of battle I let my emotions get the better of me and handled the situation poorly. I would like to thank my fans and supporters for understanding that I am human, and I look forward to continuing the journey, both professionally and personally, with you all as I move forward and grow from this experience."

What is missing? The words "sorry" or "apology" never actually appear. Admittedly, a day later she amended her press statement, apologizing to her opponent, the USTA, and tennis fans everywhere, but by then the damage had been done.

It is not only our athletes who seem to have trouble apologizing. I am sure everyone in this room recalls this summer's incident in Cambridge involving the professor and the police Sergeant, also known as "Gates-Gate." Aside from the particulars of the incident, the real story, of course, happened when our President weighed in on the matter. Realizing that his intervention had unfortunately ratcheted up a local incident to a national level, he felt compelled to weigh in a second time. Most people remember this next speech for introducing the concept of "a teachable moment" into the vernacular. I was struck by what it lacked. President Obama stated:

> I want to make clear that in my choice of words I think I unfortunately gave an impression that I was maligning the Cambridge Police Department or Sergeant Crowley specifically – and I could have calibrated those words differently. And I told this to Sergeant Crowley. I continue to believe, based on what I have heard, that there was an overreaction in pulling Professor Gates out of his home to the station. I also continue to believe, based on what I heard, that Professor Gates probably overreacted as well. My sense is you've got two good people in a circumstance in which neither of them were able to resolve the incident in the way that it should have been resolved and the way they would have liked it to be resolved.

Again, what is missing? How in the world could we expect either the professor or the officer to apologize if the President himself could not bring himself to utter the words "I'm sorry"? Our world is full of non-apology apologies. Democrats and Republicans, scholars and athletes, Popes and plain folk all acknowledge but don't apologize. Somewhere along the way the ordinary act of saying "I'm sorry" with sincerity has become beyond what we can be expected to do.

This Shabbat is *Shabbat Shuvah*. It is perhaps the most sacred Shabbat of the Jewish calendar, nestled between the New Year and Yom Kippur. These ten days are all about saying "I'm sorry." We acknowledge our shortcomings and frailties, we admit them to others as we ask their forgiveness, we apologize. According to Jewish tort law (Bava Kamma 8:7), if one injures a fellow, one can pay damages, medical bills, and every other mode of compensation, but one is not forgiven until one has given an apology. So too with our interpersonal offenses. The rabbis make very clear in Mishnah Yoma (8:9), the Mishnah that deals with Yom Kippur, that the key to unlocking the power of these days lies in a well-placed apology. Yom Kippur alone does not grant atonement, there are no magical properties to the day. The success of Yom Kippur hangs on our ability to arrive at *shul* tomorrow night, having made apologies to our loved ones, family, and community. Each one of us should be able to look back on the week gone by having issued apologies. If you can't, well the only good news is that you still have 36 hours.

There is a wonderful book called *On Apology* by Aaron Lazare, a distinguished psychiatrist who is Chancellor and Dean of the University of Massachusetts Medical Center. In the early 1990's, Lazare became intrigued by the process of apology. Lazare lists the numerous ways that we avoid saying those words. Let me offer a few:

1) We apologize, but do it without sincerity. The words come out, but they are hollow and tinny and reflect no contrition. With four young children, I know this apology well. I tell them to apologize to each other. They say, "I'm sorry," with an abject lack of sincerity. It is a start, but as adults hearing it, we know that it may be better to say nothing at all.
2) As adults, more often we employ what I call the flow-of-traffic defense. I am just doing what everyone else is doing. We justify our own inadequacies by pointing out other people's shortcomings. As Camus wrote, "To justify himself, each relies on the other's crimes."
3) A conditional apology: Janet Jackson, Arnold Schwarzenegger, this one is all over the place: "If anyone was offended by what I said, I apologize." It is the oldest trick in the book. And it is particularly offensive because it shifts the blame. The offense is no longer objective but merely a matter of perception. If you are offended, well that is your issue, but not my intention, in fact, many people may not think my action to be offensive – is it really my fault that you do?
4) A vague apology – I apologize for whatever I did. This one was made famous by Trent Lott some years ago, to apologize

for a "poor choice of words." Again, non-specific, like Serena Williams' speech, it gives the appearance of contrition, but falls short of the mark.
5) The passive apology – this is the most famous, especially in political circles. "Mistakes were made." My mistakes, not necessarily; mistakes, whom do they belong to? Not sure.

I have given you five, but I could give you fifty ways to not say sorry without apologizing. No matter which technique – each one is equally unsatisfactory, each one a mode by which we avoid what we know we have to do. We don't apologize because we think it is a sign of weakness. Our egos, our vanity, our pride, stop us from acknowledging that we were wrong and someone else was right. Moreover, when we do apologize, there is no promise of forgiveness. It is a leap of faith, and a baring of the soul. Worse than lowering ourselves in the estimation of others is the possibility that we could then have that fact lorded over us. But more than that, to apologize with sincerity, in true contrition, forces each of us to realize our own shortcomings, to admit our own guilt and shame for past misdeeds – and that is a very hard thing for any of us to do.

This leaves us, of course, with the real question. Why are apologies so important? Why do they matter as much as they do? First and foremost, apologies are important because they acknowledge a wrong that one has committed. Did you ever wonder why any support group always begins with my name is so-and-so, and I am a gambler, an alcoholic, or whatever. Because the first step in any rehabilitation process is being honest about who we are, even in our faults.

Lazare writes that a critical reason apologies are so important is that an apology is an assurance that the offended party is not at fault. Too often, the offended party questions whether they were somehow responsible for the offense. To say "I am sorry" to another person relieves that person of their concern of culpability. Apologizing has a restorative effect on both the offender and the offended.

There are other reasons, but I think the most important reason to apologize is also the most basic. We need to apologize because a sincere and well-placed apology is the key to reconciliation and healing. Not because it admits fault or makes one party feel superior to another. Apologies are important because they signal shared values in a way that enable a relationship to proceed forward. To use a trivial example, when you apologize to someone for running late for a lunch date, what you are doing in essence is identifying a common value – being on time – and acknowledging that good friends or colleagues, in a perfect universe, show up to lunch when they say they will. You apologize, because on that occasion you fell short of this ideal or standard that you share in common with your friend.

To not apologize is to say that you don't share a value system with another person. To use Lazare's language, apologies, "remind us that people can make mistakes and recover from them, that values once ignored can be reestablished, that a relationship can be healed. We breathe easier knowing that our original estimation of the offending party was correct after all; our trust was not misplaced." An apology bears with it incredible potential for healing. In a topsy-turvy world it tells us that there is a right and wrong, all is not relative, and while each of us may fall short, we all know that there is an identifiable bar to which we aspire.

There are some people in this world who think that apologies are a sign of weakness. Personally, I think that apologies are a sign of strength. It is incredibly hard to take responsibility for an error in judgment. It is hard to admit faults to ourselves and even tougher to admit them to others. But if you can't, if you can't bring yourself to utter the words "I'm sorry," then the path of *teshuvah*, of repentance, will be forever closed to you.

The midrash explains that on the eve of the very first Sabbath of creation, after creating the sun, the moon, the stars, the beasts of the field, and the fish of the sea, God went through a final punch-list of items before entering the first Sabbath. Each item God checked off makes intuitive sense, like the rainbow, the manna, the Garden of Eden. One item stands out from others in the list. The *midrash* explains that before that Sabbath, God did not rest until *teshuvah*, repentance, had been created. God knew that the world could not exist and humanity could not endure, unless we had the ability to say, "I'm sorry."

There is ultimately one reason why saying I'm sorry is so important, because it is through an apology that we can create and maintain our world – the world in which we live, the world that we seek to create in the year to come.

Yom Kippur
"Do you still love me?"

Sadie and Abe had been married for many years. Over the decades, they had built a life together, achieving great material success, living far more luxuriously than they ever imagined from their humble beginnings. One day Abe came home from work, crushed, his face downcast and ashen. He turned to his Sadie, his life partner: "Sadie, today I lost everything. Our savings, our retirement, our yacht, our home in Italy, everything... Sadie, we don't have a penny to our name. Sadie – will you still love me?" Without hesitation, Sadie turned to her Abe, saying: "Abe, I loved you from the moment we first met, I loved you when we had nothing, I have loved you every day we have been together, I love you now and I will always love you... I'll miss you."

Do you love me? Do you love me as much now as you did then? Do you love me rich or poor? In sickness and in health? Do you love me equally in my successes and my failures? If a single question could summarize the human condition, this would be it. Whether it is Sadie and Abe, or Tevye in *Fiddler on the Roof*, or any of us, no matter who we are, all of us carry around this anxiety. It is the gnawing interrogative that makes us human: Do you love me? "It may not change a thing," but as the song goes, it is sure "nice to know." It is not just that we want to be loved, we want to be loved independent of station or standing, with a love that transcends time and place, context and circumstance.

It is this question, in its various formulations, that I have heard uttered again and again this year more than any other year I can remember. Our concern, our nagging fear is that our relationships are shot through with contingencies, and that once our station in life changes, so will the affections of others. Too often in the year gone by, we have asked this question and discovered to our dismay that our lives are filled with fair-weather friends. There are people who are with us when the going is good, at our sides in our victories, full of praise in our successes, and then, we discover that nobody knows us when we're down and out.

In the past year, so many have faced this angst. While I am neither an economist nor an employment agency, in speaking to congregants, friends, and family across the country, I have learned that as disorienting as the loss of a job may be, as traumatic as the lack of financial stability is, equally injurious is the numbness one experiences on the day when the phone stops ringing. A social circle comes to a screeching halt, a sense of purpose is pulled out from under, we realize… that people love us, but maybe not for who we are, who we really are. It is a sting like no other to realize that your so-called "circle of friends" turns out not to be so present when the chips are down.

Here in this room, there are countless individuals suffering immeasurable psychological trauma from the effects of being overlooked or disregarded by those very individuals to whom they had previously been connected. Our sense of purpose, our sense of self is derailed by the effects of living in a disposable society. We live in a world where the human soul has been commoditized, each of us measured by an externally imposed sense of worth. It is not only those suffering from job loss who feel it. Our society does it to everyone. There are many alienated souls in our midst – the infirm, the handicapped, the homebound, the poor, all those who have been deemed a drain on the state, on the community, on others. The retiree, the divorcee, anyone who has found themselves estranged from their community of origin. Again and again the *mahzor* cries out – "*al na tashliheni b'et ziknah*, Do not cast me out in my old age!" Heschel explained that the what the elderly fear is not chiefly deteriorating health or human mortality, it is rejection by family and society, the fear that in frailty, we are no longer loved and needed. "Personal needs come and go," Heschel wrote, "but one anxiety remains: Am I needed? There is no man who has not been moved by that anxiety." (*Between God and Man*, p. 132)

Time and time again, our society has proven to have no stamina, no "stick-to-itude" when it comes to the relationships that bind us together. As many of you may know, next month marks the 150th anniversary of the publication of Darwin's *Origin of Species*, a book that explains why certain characteristics are more or less favorable towards adaptation and reproduction. A "who will live and who will die" minus the God part. In our free marketplace of social Darwinism, where affections are faddish and commitments ephemeral, our social fabric has taken a terrible toll. We have all served as enablers toward creating a world that lets our own sense of self and our perception of others to be derived from positions, titles, or status. Somewhere along the way, we have forgotten that the ultimate determinant to our happiness is not in a title or external trait, but here, within our core. As the great Scottish poet Robert Burns wrote, "The rank is but the guinea's stamp; the man's the gold for all that."

I think a big part of the reason that I am so aware of the manner by which a sense of self is both freely given and quickly taken by our society is that the past year has been, for me personally, a fascinating exercise on this front. I have experienced many surreal moments when I have been made deeply aware of the opportunities extended to me as Rabbi of such a distinguished congregation. The change in stationery, as it were, has opened up whole new worlds in which my phone calls are returned, a Chancellor insists on being called by his first name, a teacher becomes a colleague, I share a quiet joke with an Archbishop and a handshake with Elie Wiesel. There is something about occupying the pulpit of Steinberg, Nadich, and Lincoln that confers rank upon a man. And yes, there are some days that I do pinch myself. But in all the excitement, not a single day goes by without my knowing that these very externalities are not and can never be the measure of my self-worth. I say this not merely owing to the importance of husbanding one's vanity, not merely because my most treasured title is not "Rabbi," but "husband" and "dad." I say this because I know, as the High Holy Day prayer book teaches both you and me, *Adam yesodo mei-afar v'sofo l'afar,* man's origin is dust and his end is dust. Whether this year has brought you high or low, all of us have a common origin and all of us have a common fate. Given this great equalizer, this paradox of being both the subject of Divine concern yet of profoundly humble origins and ends, I know that the trappings of our own lives, in their comings and their goings, must never be a distraction from our real sense of self.

It's not that I don't understand the need for standing and titles – I do. My brother-in-law served as the Acting Deputy Secretary of Energy. In order to become the Deputy Secretary (and not just "Acting"), he required Senate confirmation. During the process, one Senator asked him, "You are already Acting Deputy of Energy. You are doing the job, you have the office, you have the salary and you have all the responsibilities... Does it really matter to anyone whether or not you have the full title?" To which my brother-in-law replied, "Well, yes... to my mother." For whatever reasons, admirable or otherwise, it is human nature and not necessarily wrong to seek status. But we should always remember that our lives are shaped by forces beyond our control, and we must resist hanging too much weight on that which will ultimately prove to be fleeting. None of us really know what the next stage will bring. Jerry Seinfeld once commented that there are four stages to the life of a comedian. The first stage is "Who is Jerry Seinfeld?" This is when you are starting out, when nobody knows you. The second stage is "Get me Jerry Seinfeld." This is when you are up and coming and the buzz is growing. The third is "Get me someone like Jerry Seinfeld." This is your prime. Everyone wants you, but can't get you. The final stage, as you might guess, is "Who's Jerry Seinfeld?"

Long before Seinfeld, our rabbis knew full well that we all come from the same point of origin, and that all of us will return to a common end. Perhaps each of us exists this year somewhere different on the "sine-cosine" of life, but we must not ever make the mistake of defining ourselves, or allowing ourselves to be defined, by our momentary station in life

On Rosh Hashanah I spoke of the great Israeli author Shai Agnon. There is a story told about Agnon when he learned that he had won the Nobel Prize for Literature. His friends rushed to his home to offer their congratulations. Reporters and photographers crowded into his living room to interview the writer and to take his picture. The Prime Minister and the President of the State of Israel called to wish Agnon *mazal tov*. Heads of state, artists, and writers from all over the world called or sent telegrams. At one point, a photographer asked if Agnon would sit at his desk and pretend to write something so that he could take a picture of the writer "in action." The novelist complied and wrote down a few words. After the crowd left, someone looked at the piece of paper to see what he had written. Agnon had written the five Hebrew words that I just quoted from our *mahzor: Adam yesodo mei-afar v'sofo l'afar*, Man's origin is dust and his end is dust. At the moment when he was surrounded by so much adulation, this was the simple truth that Shai Agnon felt he needed to keep in mind.

Yom Kippur is the day that we recalibrate our lens of perception, how we see each other and how we see ourselves. If we have been brought high in the past year, we look inward to make sure that we have not lost our bearings, our internal compass. If we have been brought low, then today we find ourselves affirmed knowing that in this community, here on this day, we all stand as equals before God – and equal in each other's eyes. All of us, no matter what we have experienced in the year gone by, are meant to walk into this room today, as Abe came to Sadie, as if we no longer possess all the trappings, all the externalities, all the *stuff* that defines us to ourselves and others every other day of the year. This is why we fast, this is why we wear white, this is why we recite the *viddui*, the prayer of confession said otherwise only on our death bed. All of these gestures, prayers, and rituals are meant to remind us of the day of our death. We may be dressed in our holiday finest, but inside, we should all seek to access what exists at our core, unique and sacred. The Hasidic master Rabbi Pinchas said, "in everyone there is something precious that is in no other." Today we imagine that we have only that with which we came into this world and that with which we will leave and we ask: "What is my essential core?" Once we have identified it, then we ask if we still love each other, if we love ourselves, and if we are worthy of God's love.

Go ahead... ask yourself the following. Do people like you because of your status or influence or because of your sense of values and sensibilities? My favorite essayist, Montaigne, wrote:

> If you are bargaining for a horse, you take off his trappings, you see him bare and uncovered... why in judging a man do you judge him

all wrapped up in a package? He displays to us only parts that are not at all his own, and hides from us those by which alone one can truly judge of his value. It is the worth of the blade that you seek to know, not of the scabbard...You must judge him by himself not by his finery. (Montaigne, *Essays*, Frame 189-90)

How do you greet people when you see them? When was the last time you went to visit someone in the hospital? When was the last time you made a *shiva* call? I don't begrudge anyone achievement and success. Ambition and accomplishment are values that should be preached and aspired toward. But if you have achieved success in your lifetime, I ask you to ask yourself toward what aim you are using that success. Today is Yom Kippur, you are standing alone before God, and you face your own mortality, what is it that you really stand for?

On Yom Kippur, we demand of ourselves that we be judged and judge each other by standards of enduring, if not eternal, worth. Park Avenue Synagogue, our community, must be a place where everyone feels valued, where each of us knows that were it not for him or her, this community would not be the same. I want everyone in this building and everyone associated with this institution to feel that they are being judged for the things that really matter. Whether the year gone by has raised you up or brought you low, when you walk into this building, I want you to know that your worth is measured by that which has lasting value. What are those values? Kindness, compassion, love for the Jewish community and all of humanity. The ability to say that I have given of myself according to my ability toward sustaining Jewish life. The self-satisfaction that comes with arriving at the end of every single day knowing that this world is a better place for my having been in it. I want the social networks of this community to be built on these values that transcend the particulars of any one year. I want us to love each other for who we are, knowing that we are all created in God's image and thus deserving of equal dignity. That is what I want our community to be, a place where you are recognized for what really matters, a place where you are loved for who you are inside, a place where everyone feels the joy and the responsibility that comes with the knowledge that were it not for you, we wouldn't be what we are.

This past year, I have had occasion to be present with many families upon the death of a loved one. I look around this room with the bittersweet awareness that in such a short time, we have grown close, already having cried many tears together. I have been deeply honored to be let into your lives during such raw moments of loss.

Let me tell you something that some of you already know. No matter the circumstance of death, no matter who it is, rich or poor, old or young, when I meet with the family before a funeral, I conclude every conversation with the same question. We cover biography; we discuss a person's triumphs and failures, family, profession, the relationships they held dear. We talk about just about anything a family wants to talk about. But I get the last question and it is identical for everyone: *How would your loved one want to be remembered?* After all the particulars, it is the answer to this question that I want articulated. Not for me – by then I have more than enough material to write a eulogy. I ask the question for the family. I want people to think hard about the legacy of their loved one. I want them to identify and express the values their loved one held dear, to utter them aloud, to say them around a table in each other's presence, and to acknowledge their responsibility to remember those values and pass them down.

Today is Yom Kippur – so I give you a gift, I give you a burden, I give you a question. A question that will be asked about you after your death, a question that I ask of you today on this day that we are all reminded that "our origin is dust and our end is dust": *How do you want to be remembered?*

Give it some thought, don't rush. I can think of no better way for you to spend this day of reflection and introspection than constructing your own answer. Think about it. Over the course of the day, share your answer with your loved ones. Because whatever your answer is, that is who you seek to be, at your core, in your majesty and in your simple humanity.

I have one more request. I want you to live. Live for another 120 years, but live with your answer to that question inscribed on your heart and embedded in your deeds. Live according to that answer and you will never be brought so low that you cannot recover and you will never rise so high that you forget what really matters. Live with that answer and live by that answer and you will be loved. You will be loved by those around you, you will be loved by God, and you may just love the person you become.

How do we want to be remembered? It is a question that awaits us all, it is not in your power to have it otherwise. What is in your power, what is in all our power, is to know our answer and to commit our days towards realizing our highest ideals. In doing so, each one of us will, please God, live lives worth remembering.

Sukkot
"Judaism – Universal or Particular?"

Embedded deep within the foundation of Judaism exists a tension – an anxiety wrought by an unresolved question that has been with us since our very beginning. Is our faith, our Judaism, universal or particular in its orientation? To put it another way, is our greatest concern as Jews the condition of our collective and shared humanity, or are we meant to focus on the particulars of our own peoplehood?

It is a riddle that extends all the way back to the creation of the world. Ever since the very beginning, one can find the chafing presence of both impulses, the universal and the particular. Think about it: what a strange people we are to have a calendar with not just one, but two, new years. For most other people, January is both the first month of the year and the beginning of the calendar year. We Jews alone have two – one for Jews and one for all of humanity. Rosh Hashanah, the first and second of Tishrei, marks the creation of the world. *Hayom harat olam*, "this day the world was created." It was in the beginning of Tishrei that the first person – Adam – was created: not the first Jew, but the first human being, the ancestor of collective humanity. The other new year, in Nisan, commemorates the birth of the Jewish people, their redemption from Egypt and the beginning of their peoplehood. It was in Nisan that the kings of Israel had their coronations and festivals. Even today we are prohibited from reciting certain mournful prayers during Nisan. More than any other month, Nisan celebrates the peoplehood of Israel.

Alternatively, you need look no further than today's festival, the festival of Sukkot, to see that this internal debate over Judaism as a universal or particular religion extends beyond the Bible into rabbinic literature. Every festival has a set of sacrifices, a different sacrifice for each day of the festival. The order of sacrifices codified by the Torah for Sukkot asks for a staggering total of 70 bullocks to be offered by the ancient Israelites over the course of the festival. The rabbis of the Talmud (Sukkot 55b) teach that these 70 bullocks represent the 70 nations of the world. In the rabbinic mind, Sukkot is meant to turn Israel's attention to the community of nations. Unlike the inward-looking Days of Awe, Sukkot is meant to highlight Israel's responsibility and message to the greater world.

Strikingly, elsewhere in rabbinic literature, these same 70 sacrifices are interpreted to make a very different, if not contrary, point. The 70 sacrifices are not evenly distributed, 10 per day of the festival. Nor as you might think, does the number of sacrifices increase every day. Rather, the Torah calls for 13 bullocks on the first day, 12 on the second day, and so on, one less each day, adding up to the total of 70. The rabbis construe the descending progression as a sign of God's unique relationship to Israel. They compare the decreasing number of sacrifices to the case of a king who orders his servants to prepare a great banquet. The celebration goes on for days, but as the final day of the festivities arrives, the king turns to his beloved companion and says, "make for me a small meal – so that I may enjoy your company alone." The point of this *midrash* seems to be the intimate relationship between God and Israel, and our singular status as God's chosen people.

It is not an altogether theoretical question. This week I met with the heads of two social service organizations, the American Jewish Joint Distribution Committee (JDC) – an international relief organization – and Avodah, a post-college Jewish Service Corps. Both organizations, in very different ways, understand their mission to extend within the Jewish community and beyond it. The JDC helps Jews around the world from Venezuela and Iran to Israel and the FSU, but also engages in a small percentage of projects that serve non-Jews. Avodah volunteers engage in work in the non-Jewish world, the very point being that Jewish service means service to the outside world. Is it good or bad that the mission of Jewish organizations is directed beyond the borders of the Jewish world? Does it make you feel proud or concerned to know that your Jewish philanthropic dollar may go to serve a non-Jew?

Are we inward or outward looking? It is a fascinating question, one that has always been with us, but has really come to the forefront over the last few hundred years, as Jews have become full participants in contemporary culture and society. For the first time, Jews have been concerned not only with their own condition, but with their role within the broader community. One of the most famous responses to this question was penned by Rabbi Shimshon Raphael Hirsch, who in 1836 at the age of 28 years old, wrote a slim volume entitled *The Nineteen Letters*. Hirsch was a dynamic and charismatic speaker, teacher, and leader, who eventually went on to become the founder of Modern Orthodoxy. The letters document a fictional correspondence between Naftali, a young rabbi, and Benjamin, a youthful intellectual. Naftali seeks to explain to Benjamin how a modern Jew may remain steadfast in his or her commitments to both Judaism and modern society, in other words, to explain how one can embrace a very particularistic notion of Jewish identity and also embrace all the universalism of Enlightenment Europe.

Hirsch's answer, still powerful today, is that it is not an either/or proposition. One does not have to choose between a particular and universal conception of Jewish identity. Hirsch coined the phrase "Israel-Mensch" as the ideal expression of a Jew. The Israel-Mensch is a Jew who serves humankind best by living as a Jew. To be an Israel-Mensch does not mean, as others argued, to be a Jew in the home and a secular citizen in the street. To be an Israel-Mensch means that you know how to apply the principles of your Jewish identity to the concerns of all of humanity. Neither Judaism nor humanity, Hirsch reasoned, is served by a Jew shedding his or her particular identity. Rather, humanity and Judaism are both enriched by the Jew who leverages his or her Jewishness towards the universal concerns of all of humankind.

The tragedy of the Jewish community today is that we have not internalized this notion of the Israel-Mensch. We find ourselves either entirely consumed with our own concerns or believing that we must shed our Jewishness, lest it interfere with the secular commitments we hold sacred. The philosopher Renan didn't realize the truth he had hit upon when he wrote "He who is 100% British or 100% American or 100% Russian is only half a man – the universal part of his personality, equally essential to becoming human, is still unborn." As Jews we walk a tightrope between our two identities, or more precisely, we believe that universalism and particularism are two sides of the same coin. This balancing act is perhaps best expressed at the intersection of Hillel's two classic questions: "If I am not for myself, who will be for me? And if I am only for myself, then what am I?" The point is not one question or the other, but in their juxtaposition, in the breath that we take between the two.

To be part of the chosen people means that we are chosen to serve the world by means of expressing our Jewish faith. We are a chosen people, not because we are better than others, nor because we must stand on the sidelines. We are a chosen people because within us lies a unique and particular message and mission that cries out to all people. As Zwi Werblowsky, Professor Emeritus of Religion at the Hebrew University, advised, to be Jewish is to adopt a stance exhibiting a "commitment to humanity... an openness to the world and all men." There is no greater credit to a particular religion, Judaism or other, than to place the needs of humanity at the forefront of its communal agenda. Over 100 years after Hirsch, Abraham Joshua Heschel reminded us that "no religion is an island," we are all involved with one another. "A religious man," Heschel wrote, "is a person who holds God and man in thought at one time, at all times, who suffers in himself harm done to others, whose greatest passion is compassion, whose greatest strength is love and defiance of despair." (*Moral Grandeur and Spiritual Audacity*, p. 289) Like the Sukkah itself, our Jewish communal institutions must be built in a way that provides shelter to the Jewish community, but always leaves open the ability to appreciate and express concern for the outside world.

My favorite story about Rabbi Shimshon Raphael Hirsch took place towards the end of his life. He was a deeply religious man, severe in his beliefs and punctilious in his observance, the father of German Orthodoxy if not Orthodoxy as a whole. The story is that at the end of his life, when already in frail health, Hirsch went to visit the Swiss Alps. Many people found this a strange and impulsive thing for such a learned rabbi to do. Wouldn't it be more fitting for him in his the final days to turn his attention to the people and the Torah that had sustained him throughout? So his disciples asked why he was making such a trip. He responded, "I have a feeling that after I die, and I am called in before God, one of the questions that the Almighty will ask me is: So Shimshon, you lived so close to my Alps, did you ever get a chance to see them?"

As Jews, we are a community with concerns and needs unique to us that ultimately only we will protect. But there is also a bigger world in which we exist; and as Jews, we are obligated to appreciate its beauty, to serve its needs, and not be afraid of its occupying our agenda. This is what it means to be an Israel-Mensch, to serve humanity by serving Judaism, to serve Judaism by serving humanity. This is the key to our Jewish identity, the essence of who we are, and it is towards this bar that we strive, here today and every day of the Jewish year.

Noaḥ
"Two-by-Two"

Dating has become a bit more complex since the days of Noah's Ark. Two-by-two they entered, male and female: the birds, the cattle, the creeping things – two of each to stay alive. While none of us would wish the circumstances of our *parasha* to be repeated, in retrospect, the numbers certainly took the guesswork out of choosing the right mate. In fact, all the narratives preceding the Flood have a certain mathematical charm. Adam and Eve stand together in the Garden of Eden, one fashioned from the rib of the other, their entire dating period – from courtship to consummation – consisting of a first and final date involving one piece of fruit, a snake, and just the right mixture of human shame and sexuality. When it comes to finding your *bashert*, the Book of Genesis has left little room for error.

If you are single, or if you have single friends or children, then you know that we have long ago left Eden. Things are a lot more complicated these days. Despite the growth of social networks, a liberalization of sexual mores, a leveling of historic gender imbalances, and an ever-increasing sense of geographic mobility, it is harder, not easier, to get married today than it has ever been. The availability of choices, it would seem, for both men and women, has not resulted in an increase in marital commitment, but just the opposite. According to the National Center for Health Statistics, marriage rates are dropping across the country. Those who *are* getting married, are getting married later in life; in 2006 the median age for males was 27 and for females, 25.

When we turn to the data about the Jewish community, the landscape has changed even more dramatically. Far removed from Eden, generations from the *shtetl* matchmakers, American Jews tend to marry later than Americans in general. In fact, according to the Jewish Federations of North America's last National Jewish Population Survey, proportionally fewer Jews than all Americans have ever married, especially those aged 25-34. Jewish women, the studies indicate, put off having children until later years, and then approach, but do not meet, fertility levels of all U.S. women. Jewish fertility is too low to replace the Jewish population. The data is rather stark, and while people may debate how this came to be and what to do about it, the facts are incontrovertible. What we don't know from surveys we know anecdotally. I imagine you, like I, can identify a world of single friends – Andrews and Michaels, Steves and Davids, but more often than not, Marnis and Jens, Sarahs and Emilys – bright, successful, attractive Jewish men and women who are failing to do what Adam and Eve accomplished in spite of themselves, what the couples on the Ark could not help but doing: to find each other, to commit to each other, and to create homes and families together.

This is a very sensitive topic, and it is worthy of a discussion far longer than a sermon will permit. So this morning, let me be clear both as to what I am saying and as to what I am not saying. First, what I am not saying: I am not saying that young people should be bullied into marriage against their best interest. Looking back on myself at 18 years of age, I remain astounded that I allowed that young man of such poor judgment to make decisions that still haunt the grown man that I am today. People in their post-college years are young, perhaps younger than they ever have been, and marriage is a decision of vast consequence. As important as Jewish reproductive rates are, so are happy families. So too, I am not talking about divorce rates; that is also a sermon for another day. But in my line of work, I know of enough instances of people making the difficult, but important, decision to end a dysfunctional marriage. We would all do well to remember that divorce, however painful, has been an option for many, including some in this room, who are very thankful for it. I also want to make clear, that while I do believe marriage is a value that should be preached and encouraged, our community, both here at Park Avenue Synagogue and beyond, must be a community that validates the integrity of our unmarried members. The organized Jewish community has an unfortunate proclivity to run roughshod over unmarrieds, to make single Jews feel they have a lesser status than their partnered contemporaries. From our membership forms to our programming, I expect our synagogue to model a religious life that embraces all of its members equally regardless of marital status.

What I am asking you to consider is that right now we are living through a perfect storm of sociological factors that have collectively resulted in a state of affairs in which two Jews who, in principle, favor the institution of marriage are disinclined to take that step. Let me list a few of the elements: American Jewish women stand out for their high level of educational attainment. Our daughters, mine included, are extended the same professional training, opportunities, and advancement as their male counterparts. While we can take rightful joy in this development, unheard of in previous generations, there are also consequences to the choice of postponing marriage and childbearing due to graduate school and professional development. Another element: Jewish men and women, once excluded from fully blending into the melting pot of America, now find themselves taken in with open arms by willing non-Jewish partners. The libidinal anxieties surrounding the Jewish-Gentile encounters of Woody Allen's *Annie Hall*, or Philip Roth's *Portnoy's Complaint*, seem totally passé to young Jews of today. If you put this all together, and throw in the implications of the birth control pill... well, it doesn't take a genius to reflect on how different the world is now than it was fifty years ago.

Each of these factors – educational achievement, acceptance in secular society, and reproductive choice – is cause for celebrating, and to speak very directly, worthy of vigorous defense. But we can't act as if the playing field is the same as it was fifty years ago. We can't feign surprise when Jews in their late 30's and older find themselves wondering when their *bashert* will arrive. Our problem, quite simply, is that in our excitement over advancing a series of agendas we have forgotten to consider the hidden implications of these changes. I am reminded of the decision of the Jewish Theological Seminary to ordain women as Rabbis and Cantors after months and years of politicking and debate. Women students arrived and only then did anyone realize that with all the deliberations and planning, nobody had thought to build new women's bathrooms. Our intent has been admirable; our failure has merely been one of not thinking everything through.

I should also note that our present discussion is not altogether new. I recall one of the first pages of Talmud I ever studied contained a debate on the recommended order of events when it comes to Torah study and marriage. One opinion holds that one should study Torah first and then get married. After all, how could one possibly be focused on one's intellectual development while occupied with the concerns and burdens of family life. The other side argues that one should first get married and only then commit oneself to Torah study, because how on earth, Rashi asks, can one be devoted to professional development while absorbed and distracted by thoughts of finding a mate. (B.T. Kiddushin 29b) While our sages only ever discussed the issue vis-à-vis the men's choice, the debate – as we all know – is far more intense for women, when it comes to juggling career and family. As a female friend of mine pointed out to me this week, when it comes to family and career, there is an inescapable difference between men and women. As she put it, while men may live their lives simultaneously, women more often than not, lead their lives sequentially.

Since arriving at Park Avenue Synagogue, I have tried to raise the big issues, the conversations that will shape the future of our immediate community and of American Jewry: Congregational School, Shabbat Services, and Israel, to name a few. But to state the obvious, all these conversations are only relevant with the first operating assumption in place – the presence of Jews. If there are no Jews being born into this world, everything else is – as they say – gravy.

There are, just a few blocks east of here, more unaffiliated young Jews than you can shake a stick at. Park Avenue Synagogue, rightly so, has primary responsibilities to its membership. I do believe, however, that when it comes to outreach vs. inreach, it is not an either/or proposition. To be a forward-looking synagogue, we need either to create programs for these unaffiliated young Jews or to partner with the organizations best-positioned to ensure a Jewish future. I want the names and email addresses of every post-Birthright twenty-something on the East Side. I want the alumni associations of Brandeis, Penn, Michigan, Harvard – any college with a strong Jewish alumni base in New York City – to know that the doors of this synagogue are open to their members. I want young adults to feel that there is a place in the Jewish world for them to meet, to socialize, to learn, to pray, and maybe even find a mate. I want them to feel like *this* synagogue is a place where that can happen. It is a discussion to which I am committed and I look for your ideas and support towards making it happen.

Even more than in the synagogue, it is in our own homes that we need to give careful attention to this issue. We need to find the vocabulary to communicate to our children the inestimable value of creating a Jewish family. We need to communicate that while we prize academic and professional achievement, while we value the integrity of every person *as an individual*, we also are encouraging and proud of their choice to get married. We need to be honest with our children about the internal contradiction of sending them off to liberal arts colleges, telling them to study whatever they want, become whoever they want to be, make friendships with as diverse a circle as possible, but when it comes to bringing someone home, he or she better be Jewish. Even with internal contradictions we should be candid about our expectations, and calculated in our planning. We need to use language that lets our children know that while every human being is created equally in God's image, the importance of creating a Jewish home, with two Jewish partners, by birth or by conversion, is the starting point for a discussion of a Jewish future. I readily admit that as a father, I myself am working on what this conversation should look like, but as a Rabbi, I can think of no conversation more important to cultivate within each of our households.

There is a wonderful midrash that tells of a conversation between Rabbi Yossi and a Roman matron. The Roman matron asked Rabbi Yossi what God has been doing since creating the world. She was astounded when Rabbi Yossi told her that ever since Creation, God was preoccupied with matchmaking. "Why, how could that be so difficult?" she remarked, "I myself could do it." The Roman matron turned Yenta and lined up a thousand male servants opposite a thousand maidservants – "You marry her, you marry him" – matching them all up in one night. The next morning, disaster was evident all around – a bruise here, a cut there, broken limbs and black eyes. She asked them, "What happened?" This one said, "I don't want him" and that one said, "I don't want her." The matron had to admit that there was no God like the God of Israel for truth. (Gen. Rab. 68:4) The punchline of the story: "It is as difficult for God to match a couple as it was to split the Red Sea."

It isn't easy being a matchmaker. It probably never was. It is a challenge for God, and it is certainly a challenge for us. But it is the task on which all other Jewish conversations depend. We are not the first to have this conversation, but if we want to make sure that we are not the last, then we must have it, and have it honestly. We need to look at the landscape of the wider community and provide a response in tune with our age. We need to define our synagogue's responsibilities beyond the borders of present membership with an eye towards our future membership. Most importantly, each of us in our own home needs to engage in the 'Godlike' task of creating Jewish couples, two by two, sailing bravely towards our Jewish future.

Toldot

"Judaism: Liberal or Conservative?"

I would hope that when asked for help by a brother in need, each of us in this room would respond better than our patriarch Jacob did. The scene is one we know well: Esau comes home, famished from a hunt. He is faint and believes himself to be near death; he begs his brother for a bowl of lentil soup. Unconscionably, Jacob responds by demanding something in return – the birthright. Esau, in all his flawed humanity, responds: "I am at the point of death, so of what use is my birthright to me?" (Gen. 25:32) He sells his birthright on the spot. The deal secure, Jacob feeds Esau, a bitter meal shared between brothers.

So much for the first Jewish soup kitchen.

What would you have done? What do you do? How do you respond when asked for help by someone in need? As Jews with liberal sensibilities, we squirm at the way Jacob responded, a charitable act done so grudgingly. Yet, you and I both know that that we can't and don't give to everyone in need. It is not only because we are unsure as to whether that homeless person will use the dollar for food or for drugs. We don't give, or – let me speak personally – *I* don't always give, because while supporting the needy is unequivocally a Jewish value, resources are limited and there are different strategies when it comes to expressing that value. You don't have to be an economist to know that when addressing societal ills, the most effective remedy isn't necessarily giving out dollar after dollar. I feel the anxiety everyday – not just on the street, but here in the building. As rabbi of a synagogue called "Park Avenue Synagogue," I receive numerous requests for *tzedakah* every single day, in person, by email, by mail, by phone. Should I give to everyone who asks, or should I write a large check to FEGS or Met Council or one of the other agencies that work towards providing self sufficiency? Shall we be the sort who give out fish, or teach people how to fish? The question goes beyond local acts of charity. What about the bigger concerns facing the nation – poverty, housing, or more currently, health care? When it comes to setting social policy, does Judaism recommend one approach over another? Are Jews, is Judaism, liberal or conservative in its orientation?

Over the past few months there has been a rather fascinating and occasionally vitriolic public debate taking place between Norman Podhoretz of *Commentary* and Leon Wieseltier of *The New Republic*, addressing the question of Jews and social policy. While this debate has been going on for quite a while, it has taken on new life with Podhoretz's latest book *Why Are Jews Liberal?* Podhoretz explores why Jews have historically aligned themselves with liberal causes, social policy, the Democratic Party – often acting and voting against our self-interest, recalling Milton Himmelfarb's quip that "Jews earn like Episcopalians and vote like Puerto Ricans." Podhoretz, the champion of neo-conservatives, argues that while it made sense to be an economic liberal when Jews were starving over sewing machines in the sweatshops of the Lower East Side, there is no defensible reason for Jews to continue to cluster on the political left, chasing the false messiah of liberalism. Making things all the more awkward, when it comes to Israel, it has been the political right, not the political left, that has proven time and time again to be the staunchest supporters of Israel. Podhoretz and his neo-conservative Jewish colleagues like the late Irving Kristol write essays with gentle titles like "On the Political Stupidity of Jews." They are exasperated by their brethren who continue to flock to the left, against their own interests, against Israel's interests, and against any accurate reading of Jewish tradition.

Then comes Wieseltier, the champion of the Jewish left, perplexed by Podhoretz's bafflement. Is it so hard to understand, he asks, that Jews should find it difficult to swallow the Right's position on gun control, abortion, and gay rights, not to mention health care, government, and tax policy? It isn't so hard; in fact it is quite easy to open up any Jewish text and see that we are commanded to perform acts of social justice. Self-interest has never been the motivating force for what we do as Jews. We are kind to the stranger, to the orphan, to the widow and the poor, because we were once strangers in a strange land. Long ago, the Torah acknowledged that there may come a time when acts of random kindness would not necessarily be in the self-interest of the Jewish community. Our Jewish consciousness and conscience have been driven not by self-interest, but by historical memory. Whether lovers of Israel belong to the right or the left, Wieseltier takes Podhoretz to task for misreading history, misreading the motivations of the Christian Right and mistakenly believing that it is somehow a contradiction for a Jew to love Israel and have sympathy for the Palestinians. It is neither a mystery nor a scandal for Wieseltier to understand why Jews are liberal. We're liberal – as the title of Wieseltier's most recent article states – "Because we Believe."

Now I could go on. I really love these public debates. I read both authors; both *Commentary* and *The New Republic* sit on my bedside table. I read them both and then rinse thoroughly with *The New Yorker*. I figure the truth is always somewhere in between Wieseltier and Podhoretz. Which is why, of course, Jews are somewhat split as a people and as individuals when it comes to social policy. We acknowledge there is truth on both sides. We want to be liberals, but we also know there are limits. We believe in the infinite dignity of every human being, but we also know, to paraphrase Milton Friedman, that there is a time when equality of opportunity and equality of rights may not translate into material equality. If this is the case, if as the Talmud states, *"Elu v'elu,"* there is truth to both, then where does it leave us? What exactly are we to do?

I think in this conversation one needs to separate values from tactics. Let's take for obvious example what is being debated on the Senate floor today: health care. Here I rely on my teacher and rabbi, Elliot Dorff, who has written extensively on this topic. There is nothing wrong with saying that from a Jewish point of view, the fact that more than 40 million Americans have no health insurance is "an intolerable dereliction of society's moral duty." As Jews, we can be united in saying this present condition cannot continue.

Nevertheless, the Jewish demand to make health care accessible does not necessarily mandate a particular form of delivery. Judaism does not recommend the platform of one political party over another.

As the son and the brother of physicians, I am happy to say that the Talmud writes, "A physician who charges nothing is worth nothing!" (Baba Kamma 85a) Rabbinic literature has a fairly developed sense of market rates and valuing skilled labor. At the same time, you don't need to look very far in rabbinic literature to see that the entire community is responsible for ensuring that all its members receive the health care they need. Judaism holds certain values sacred; it does not recommend particular policies for realizing those values. We should be suspect of anyone who insists it does. During the years I lived in Chicago, legislation was proposed requiring that every big box store, such as Walmart or Costco, pay a certain wage with certain benefits. Every rabbi was asked to preach in favor of passing that legislation. The effect of the legislation, well meaning as it was, was the opening of new Walmart stores, but on the other side of the state border. Because of the legislation, the jobs and the consumers went five minutes further down the road, taking a lot of tax dollars away, tax dollars that presumably would have gone to pay for some of the pressing social service needs of Illinois.

I have no problem giving a sermon that will make me unpopular with anyone or everyone in the room. If you want to know what I think about health care, or governmental intervention, or tax policy – you can invite me for a beer – I have an opinion just as each of you do. But from this pulpit, I won't tell you that Judaism teaches X, Y, or Z about it. I won't, because it is intellectually dishonest to say that it does.

Judaism is not liberal or conservative; it is neither and it is both. This acknowledgment signals the beginning, not the end of the conversation. When you find yourself struggling to respond to health care or the minimum wage or a homeless person on the street, don't despair. Your anxiety means that you are human. If you weren't concerned about health care, if you weren't concerned about the plight of the homeless, *then* you should worry. The most critical part of this conversation is that you do not let your angst lead to inertia. This is not a theoretical exercise. It is not OK to read *Commentary* one night and *The New Republic* the next night and do nothing during the day. You must do something, whether it is giving *tzedakah* generously, giving of your time towards a volunteer organization, or being involved in the political process. A great way to start is by turning out tomorrow for our own Vicki K. Wimpfheimer Mitzvah Day. Sign up for a project, make a site visit; there are plenty of activities to choose from. Just don't stay home, tomorrow or in the days to come. It makes no difference to me if your response is liberal or conservative, I only insist that you have a response, one in which you believe and one upon which you act.

We find in the Palestinian Talmud in *Hagigah* (2:1) the following statement: "This teaching is like two paths, one of fire and one of snow. If one inclines to this side, one dies by fire; to that side, and one dies by snow. What should one do? Walk in the middle." When it comes to the issues of the day, we can be singed by the right or the left. But we dare not stand still, we dare not stand idly by, we are obligated to step forward on that path, however narrow it may be. Make no mistake, our world is deeply flawed, and we must work to repair it. We can debate the tactics, but on the goals we stand united. Today, tomorrow, and the next day we will work together towards perfecting God's creation.

Va-yetzei
"Jewish and American"

Of the 52 *Shabbatot* of the Jewish year, Shabbat Thanksgiving may not rank at the very top of the hierarchy. Many people are away, and those of us who are here feel the lingering side effects of the last two days of food... and relatives. Certainly, when compared to *Shabbat Shuvah*, between Yom Kippur and Rosh Hashanah, or *Shabbat Hagadol*, just before Passover, Shabbat Thanksgiving is a strictly American and relatively recent phenomenon. That said, for us in the room, I think that this Shabbat, perhaps more than any other Shabbat of the year, is deeply important, in that it alerts us to the two calendars by which we live: the secular or civic time of Thanksgiving, and the Jewish rhythms of Shabbat and festivals. This weekend forces us to consider what it is to be part of both traditions. Moreover, on this Shabbat, we have students in from college, products of our community, back to see family and back today to check in on the synagogue in which they grew up. It is to this audience, the liberal arts crowd, past, present, or future, that I direct my thoughts today. I want to think aloud with you about what it means to be part of both a campus culture and Jewish tradition – a hyphenated identity with a foot in two worlds. A bit of a disclaimer up front: as with the twisted professorial path of some of your college lectures, there may be a moment or two when you wonder where I am heading. I can't promise you that every moment will make perfect sense, but at the very least, rest assured there is no exam at the end.

Last month, the great French anthropologist Claude Lévi Strauss died at the age of 100. His death prompted me to dust off some of his books from my freshman Intro to Anthropology class. Lévi Strauss spent his career studying cultural systems from different continents and eras, comparing everything from kinship systems, marriage rules, rituals of all kinds, and mythological narratives. Over the course of his career, he came to the conclusion that "the human mind is everywhere one and the same and that it has the same capacities." His book *The Savage Mind* argues that, notwithstanding certain contextual differences, there really aren't any differences between the primitive mind and the civilized mind. Lévi Strauss's research tallies the cultural tropes shared across civilizations, what he called "the search for the invariant." So, for instance, something common to many mythologies is a cosmology with a central vertical axis that connects the sky and the earth, variously symbolized as the world pole, the sacred mountain, the church steeple, or as we read this morning, Jacob's ladder. The cosmologies may differ in particulars, but they reflect a universal element of mythology – Shamanistic, Biblical, or otherwise.

From reading Lévi Strauss, I went on to read a fascinating book that put him into conversation with two other thinkers from our college reading list, Freud and Marx. *The Ordeal of Civility* is by John Murray Cuddihy, a member of the faculty at CUNY. His thesis is altogether intriguing. Cuddihy reflects on the intellectual legacy of Lévi Strauss, Freud, and Marx, pointing out that these giants of anthropology, psychology, and economics are all of Jewish descent. Freud and Marx's Jewishness are the subject of much scholarship, and Lévi Strauss, though never a practicing Jew, was the grandson of a Rabbi in Versailles and recalled being called a "dirty Jew" in grade school.

Cuddihy argues out that each one of these famous diaspora Jewish intellectuals was involved in a lover's quarrel with the modern world. Each of them epitomizes Bernard Rosenberg's definition of a Jewish intellectual as someone "who pretends to have forgotten his Yiddish." Marx's father had converted, while Freud and Lévi Strauss never had an open break. No matter what their Jewish background, each of them developed an ideological strategy by which to transcend their Jewishness. Freud's psychoanalysis sought to identify those conditions that were common across ethnic cultures and ethnic lines: the unconscious, the taboos, the confrontations with guilt, shame, and sexuality. So too, Marx's communism sought to deny or transcend economic differences often associated with a bourgeois Jewish trading class. Lévi Strauss, as I noted, made his name by pointing out that religions all have the same goal and while differing on tactics, share far more than they otherwise acknowledge.

Each thinker, according to Cuddihy, kicked Judaism upstairs, escaping upward into a more refined level of the cultural system. They, or at least Lévi Strauss and Freud, refused to formally assimilate. They leveled the playing field, creating disciplines that made Jewish problems, and the Jewish people, universal. In other words, each of the disciplines they created enabled Jews to be full participants in a secular world without having to wear their Judaism on their sleeves.

You see, whether it is Marx and Freud, or you and I, the modern Jew is faced with a very basic problem. How does one acknowledge the particularity of our Jewish origins and, at the same time, claim to be a full participant in civic society? There are many answers to this question, often called "The Jewish Question." Theodore Herzl saw the desire for Jews to be like all other people and their inability to do so in Europe, so he founded political Zionism, believing a Jewish state to be the only way for Jews to be both Jews and citizens of the world. Chabad, or the Ba'al Teshuvah movement, rejects modernity, or at least the intellectual claims that modernity presents. In a sense, Conservative, Reform, and Orthodox Judaism all represent different modes by which a Jew negotiates his or her place in Jewish and secular culture. Cuddihy's thesis seems to be suggesting that the fathers of western culture and the modern liberal arts education represent another path. Each one recoiled at the thought of the Jew being a social pariah, and responded by transforming all the distinguishing characteristics of being Jewish, cultural and psychological, into shared features of a diverse and variegated humanity. Modernity, in the words of Sartre in his *Anti-Semite and Jew*, brought with it a passion for the universal, where "there is no French truth or German truth...no Negro truth and or Jewish truth." Freud, Marx and Lévi Strauss, were champions of the universal, in service to their disciplines, but also in response to their awkward status as Jews in the modern world.

All this is interesting – I hope. But this is not a college classroom, it is a synagogue and, in the intimacy of this partisan crowd, there is a very practical and troubling question lingering beneath the surface. When we send our kids off to college, what sort of identity are we hoping they will create? If *you* are in college, what sort of identity are *you* seeking to create? You go to college, you take anthropology, psychology, and economics, you room with people of different faiths, traditions, and ethnic backgrounds, coming from exotic places called "the suburbs." On the one hand, one point of sending your children to college (or going to college) is to see that your children (or you) are part of a diverse landscape of varied religions and backgrounds. Your Bible, your rituals, your Jewishness is but another club at the Student Union. Now let's all go cheer for the same football team. On the other hand, if the Jewish graduates of a liberal arts college believe their Judaism to be no more and no less significant than any other cultural markers, then what exactly makes Jewish identity worth preserving?

I meet, with increasing regularity, children of this congregation who have fallen in love with non-Jews, and either at their own volition or at the prompting of a parent, we sit in my office and discuss their relationship. Not once has any of these Jewish kids expressed a disdain for Judaism, or for that matter, has the non-Jewish partner recoiled at their potential spouse's Jewishness. Nearly every couple says something to the effect of "I am a good ethical person, so is she. One of us is Jewish, the other is Catholic or Protestant or something else... Rabbi, we are two good people in love – what exactly is so complicated here?" We live in a curious and delightful and terrifying time where the anxiety wrought by the vexing Jewish question has been replaced by something more frightening – indifference.

Unless we are able to ask and answer the question of Jewish particularity, both respecting the diversity of humanity, *and* insisting on the unique contribution of Judaism to humanity, a contribution without which humanity will be irreparably impoverished, a contribution worth standing up for, fighting for and marrying for, well, then the simple truth is that we are dead in the water. We need an answer for those couples in my office, your children, and the thousands who never even bother to make an appointment. Freud, Marx, and Lévi Strauss may have been plenty smart, but with all due respect, they are not Jewish role models. I don't want to create Jews whose very success drives them to transcend their Jewishness. I want to create Jews who are able to wrestle all night with modernity, letting our sparring partner of secularism go at the moment we emerge victorious, at the moment we emerge named as Israel.

One final story, not from psychology, not from anthropology, nor from economics, but from Law. I heard it first by way of Rabbi Mitchell Wohlberg. It is the story of Justice Louis Brandeis in law school and his induction into the Harvard Honor Society. It had not been an easy road for Brandeis. For the past three years, other students – uninvited – had sat next to him as he ate lunch every day, saying things like "Brandeis, you're brilliant, you could end up on the Supreme Court – except that you are a Jew. Why don't you convert? Then all your problems will be solved." Brandeis had listened but had not responded. Finally, in his senior year of law school, his preeminence could not be denied. Jewish or not, he was invited to join the "Honor Society." On the evening of the official induction, the atmosphere was thick. All eyes were on him as he walked to the lectern. Slowly he looked around the room and began to speak; "I'm sorry I was born a Jew," he said. With that, the room erupted in applause, in an explosion of shouting and cheers. They had convinced him, they thought. They had prevailed upon him at last. Brandeis waited. When silence was regained he began again. "I am sorry I was born a Jew, but only because I wish I had the privilege of choosing Judaism on my own." This time there was no shouting, no explosion, no cheers, this time there was respectful silence. The members of the society listened attentively, awed by his strength of conviction and strength of character, by his unequivocal choice. When he finished, they gave him a standing ovation.

This story may be apocryphal. It is told without corroboration. It is a story about positive identification, how one Jew was able to negotiate his professional and secular ambitions and emerge with his Jewish identity intact and a source of welling pride. It is a story worth repeating, a story worth seeking to replicate in our own lives and the lives of our children. To see Judaism not as something to shirk or transcend, not as a choice among equals, but as a birthright worthy of transmission, worthy of struggle, worthy of celebrating. May that story be our story for generations to come.

Va-yishlaḥ
"Wars of Necessity, Wars of Choice"

What is the difference between a war of necessity and a war of choice? Judaism is not a pacifist tradition; it has always acknowledged that war, however tragic, is at times inevitable and necessary. "There is a time for loving and a time for hating, a time for war and a time for peace," teaches Ecclesiastes. Peace is our greatest blessing, we prize it and we must seek it and pursue it. However, whether you are acting in self defense or responding to the commandment not to stand idly by as your brother's blood is shed, war is a fact of life. There are times when military intervention is a moral obligation, and the decision not to do anything is actually less defensible, more reprehensible than the horrors of war.

This past week we heard of our nation's plans to increase our commitment in Afghanistan and, inevitably, increase the number of young lives at risk and lost in war. Many of us have been pondering the thorny question of when war is necessary and when it is a choice. If it is indeed necessary, if there is a threat or an evil of such a degree that we must act, our sacrifice is justified. But, if it is merely a choice, an option among others, we are left wondering if it is worth the lives lost. If it isn't a necessary war, is it worth even a single human life, a life, which as Jews, we know to be of infinite value?

This question, whether war is necessary or whether it is a choice, is not new to our age. It is this very tension that impels our *parasha* this week, specifically, the story of Dinah. It is a painful story, a story made more famous in recent years by Anita Diamant's treatment in *The Red Tent*. Depending on how you read the text, Jacob's daughter Dinah is either raped, seduced, or a willing partner of Shechem.

Shechem's heart cleaves to Dinah and he seeks her hand in marriage. By any account, such a thing is not done in Israel. It is an outrage that an outsider should sleep with a daughter of Jacob. Jacob's family responds in two very different ways. Jacob stays his hand and bides his time, even when Shechem's father, Hamor, seeks out Jacob to arrange a marriage between their children, a union between the tribes. Dinah's brothers, however, are not interested in any rapprochement. In guile, they direct the men of Shechem to be circumcised, and, as they are convalescing, Simeon and Levi lead their troops on an ambush – a full-scale punitive war. They kill the men, plunder the camp, retrieve Dinah, and return home. The most intriguing scene, the punchline of the story, is saved for the end. Jacob castigates his sons as they return from battle: "You have brought trouble on me," Jacob scolds them, "you have made me odious to the inhabitants of the land… I am few in number and they may gather against me and I will be destroyed." (Gen. 34:30) Yet, it is not Jacob, but his sons who get the last word. The tale concludes with a hanging interrogative that one cannot help but think is not only the thoughts of Simeon and Levi, but of the author of the Torah itself, a piercing question that lingers even today: "Shall he treat our sister as a whore?!" (Gen. 34:31)

The poles of the debate are set. Jacob, both then and throughout his life, sought to compromise, maneuver, accommodate, and negotiate. He may have been agitated and distraught on account of Dinah, but as the head of the household he did not want to take up arms, he wanted to resolve this conflict without bloodshed. For the aggrieved brothers of Dinah, Simeon and Levi, this was a black and white issue. For them, this was a war of necessity. Perhaps because the affront was too great, perhaps because they felt that Dinah was being held captive against her will, perhaps… For whatever reason, there was no option for the brothers in the matter. War of choice or war of necessity? The answer is not clear, but your answer to the question reveals your sympathies. By one account, the brothers' actions are just and even noble. Read otherwise, they are hotheaded, bloodthirsty, and scandalous.

For a people who lived without land and without a military for thousands of years, Jews have a surprisingly large amount to say about this topic. The biblical sources, as I have noted, acknowledge that sometimes justice requires violence. Peace is our ultimate goal, but we do not live in a messianic age. One should, according to the Torah, always offer terms of peace before attack. During battle itself, one must conduct a siege in a specific manner so as to allow for post-war reconstruction. War, tragic and horrific, must be guided by ethics, both during war and beforehand, in establishing the conditions by which war may be justified.

The thirteenth-century sage Maimonides distinguished between obligatory wars (*hovah*) and discretionary wars (*reshut*). The former are wars waged by the king in service either to God's command or in self-defense, "to deliver Israel from the enemy attacking them." The second kind of war is a discretionary conflict "to extend the borders of Israel and establish a king's greatness and prestige." For contemporary purposes, the distinction delineates the difference between wars that receive the sanction of our tradition and those that do not. It is a distinction between understanding the actions of Simeon and Levi as necessary and therefore just, or as optional and thus reprehensible.

The problem is that it all comes down to interpretation – these are very subjective distinctions. The most limiting interpretation, and here I rely on my teacher Rabbi Elliot Dorff, is offered by the rabbinic sage Judah Ibn Tibbon, who reasoned that only when the enemy is actively taking Jewish lives and the high priest approves, is war sanctioned. At the other end of the spectrum are the sages who reason that when a community merely fears attack, pre-emptive strikes are legitimate. Even more surprisingly, one commentator explains that hostilities are permissible to instill fear in potential military aggressors. (E. Dorff, *To Do The Right and The Good*, pp. 161-183)

To make matters more complicated, from the time of the Maccabees until the establishment of Israel in 1948 no Jew ever had to actively apply this wide spectrum of positions to Jewish life. Israeli Prime Minister Menachem Begin acknowledged that for Israel there were indeed wars of choice and wars of no alternative. Interestingly, he designated only the War of Independence, the war of attrition in the late 1960's and the Yom Kippur War as wars of necessity. The Six Day War, surprisingly, he called a war of choice, explaining "while it is indeed true that the closing of the Straits of Tiran was an act of aggression, a *causus belli*, there is always room for a great deal of consideration as to whether it is necessary to make a *causus* into a *bellum*." Both within Israel and the pro-Israel community there are deep divisions over these distinctions. As we witness the increasing nuclear capabilities of Iran, as Israel takes action to defend herself against terror, we must keep these distinctions in mind. Dr. Richard Haass, President of the Council of Foreign Relations, writes in his book, *War of Necessity, War of Choice*, "Wars of necessity do not require assurances that the overall results of striking or resisting will be positive. Only the assessment that the results of not so doing will be unacceptably large and negative." (Haass p. 10) It is both intolerable and unsustainable to exist, like Dinah, vulnerable to the whims of your captors. The decision to do nothing must be understood as a choice – perhaps wise, perhaps not – but like all choices, one with consequences.

As American Jews debating the policy of our secular country, we must recognize that while our tradition may inform our values system, it does not provide black and white answers. World War II, the Korean War, Vietnam, Bosnia, Kosovo – some are easy to categorize; some are hard. Should there have been military intervention in Rwanda in 1994? What about Darfur today? Should America go to war for humanitarian reasons? Should we go to war to further our democratic ideals? Do we go to war to secure resources upon which our national security depends?

When it comes to Afghanistan, many of the reasons for involvement have been discussed this week; in fact, Dr. Haass outlined some of them in a recent article. (*Washington Post*, 10/11/2009) Afghanistan is a haven for terrorists plotting against America. Afghanistan is a "human rights nightmare." To leave Afghanistan is to leave a region destabilized, bearing the potential to escalate to a nuclear confrontation. I am sure there are many reasons, but at the end of the day I am not a political scientist nor a military strategist and nobody has the gift of prophecy. There is no foolproof way to determine whether these considerations make Afghanistan presently a war of choice or a war of necessity. We gather data and opinion and hope that our leaders make informed decisions, always prizing the infinite value of human life. Even then, as with the story of Dinah, years later we will still argue over who was right and who was wrong.

This coming Friday night marks the beginning of Hanukkah. It is as close as we come as Jews to celebrating a military victory – the courage, self-sacrifice, and, ultimately, the victory of the Maccabees. This year, we will light our Hanukkah *menorah* with a tinge of sadness, knowing that yet again, as Jews, as Zionists, and as Americans we live in an era when the reality of war, the story of Hanukkah, is a bit too contemporary, a bit too close to home. I would like one day to look at the flickering flames of the *menorah* in the company of children and grandchildren with the military associations of the festival outdated and distant, theoretical and abstract. That day has yet to come. We continue to parse when wars are and are not necessary. May it be God's will that one day, in the not-too-distant future, our children will live in a world where such questions are irrelevant, such sermons immaterial, a day when as the prophet promised, "Swords shall be beaten into plowshares, and spears into pruning hooks: when nation shall not lift up sword against nation and neither shall they learn war any more." (Isaiah 2:4)

Va-yeishev
"The Joseph Generation"

Some time ago, I had the pleasure of being escorted to *shul* by my daughter. There is no greater pleasure in my life than to walk to synagogue with one of my kids. As we walked hand-in-hand, I was struck by the power of our time together and the memories it evoked. I turned to her and said, "You know what, here we are walking to *shul* together, and when I was a little boy, I remember walking to *shul* with your grandpa, my daddy. You want to know what is even more interesting, when Grandpa was a little boy, he used to walk to *shul* with his daddy." As soon as I'd said it, I was totally confident that she was totally uninterested in what I found to be so fascinating, but she gave me a response that was as pure and delightful as it was unexpected. She looked at me and asked, "Daddy, did Moses walk to *shul* with his children?" It was a wonderful question and I was touched by it, so much so, that I simply responded, "Yes, Moses walked to shul with his children."

What are the Jewish memories that you carry around? The activities, the rituals, the walks to *shul*, the teachers, the music, the trips, the tastes and smells that make up your Jewish past? Is there a tablecloth you use from a previous generation? A recipe, a *tallis*, a *Kiddush* cup that has been passed down? When I begin to deliver a sermon, I often think of Mr. Gendon, the man who I sat next to in *shul* growing up who used to hand me a peppermint candy whenever the rabbi began to speak. Maybe for you it is a blessing at the Friday night table, or a prayer when you went to sleep at night, or a bad joke that an uncle said year in and year out at the Passover *Seder*. You may be new to Judaism and your memories more recent, like the moment when you immersed in the *mikveh*, emerging a member of the Jewish people. We all have these memories, new or old. They are the fabric of who we are as Jews. Consciously or unconsciously, it is Jewish memory that drives our Jewish identity. In some cases, if we dig deep enough, our memories go back to way before we were born, sometimes even as far as Moses.

This week, the Jewish world lost one of its greatest scholars. Professor Yosef Yerushalmi, the Salo Baron Professor of Jewish History, Culture, and Society at Columbia University, passed away at the age of 77. A historian of the first rank, Yerushalmi addressed every area from the Spanish expulsion and modern German Jewry to Freud's relationship with his Judaism. With the sad news of his passing, and to honor his life, I want to speak this morning about what is probably his most famous book, a short but provocative volume entitled *Zakhor: Jewish History and Jewish Memory*. Published just over 25 years ago, *Zakhor* continues to generate discussion today. It is a slim volume, just 100 pages, and is striking both for its insights and readability. If you are going somewhere over winter break, then I suggest you pick up a copy for your holiday reading.

The thesis of the book is straightforward. Yerushalmi argues that "History" and "Memory" are two entirely different projects. History is the account of past events, personalities, and institutions. To the extent that that he or she is able, the historian seeks to separate fact from fiction and to reconstruct and record objectively "what actually happened." History is the effort to describe and explain the past.

For Jews, however, our natural reflex, our "go-to place" is not history, but memory. According to Yerushalmi, and this point is debated among scholars, Jewish history as a discipline is a relatively new phenomenon. History is not indigenous to our people; in fact, Jews only learned how to do history from their non-Jewish counterparts. Memory, on the other hand, is part of our people's DNA. The Hebrew word for "memory" or "to remember," *zakhor*, appears in the Bible no less than 169 times. Over and over again, Israel is commanded to remember and not forget; *remember* the promise to Abraham, *remember* that we were once slaves in Egypt, *remember* the Sabbath day, *remember* what Amalek did to us. The command to remember is absolute, persistent, and extends well beyond the Bible. Think of the rituals and recitals of the Passover Haggadah: "My father was a wandering Aramean," and *Dayenu* – an account of everything God did for us. These are ritualized exercises aimed at the formation of collective memory. (*Zakhor*, p. 5ff.)

Yerushalmi explains that memory, unlike history, is far more than an account of the past. History requires detachment; memory has immediacy. Memory means that you see yourself as part of a link in a chain, extending to the past, but also into your future. The story you are telling is not just any story, but *your* story. When we say at the Passover *seder* that we see ourselves as if we went out of Egypt, or on Shavuot that each of us was present at the giving of the Torah at Mount Sinai, these are not historical claims but claims of memory. Over this festival of Hanukkah, we thank God for miracles and deliverance *bayamim ha-hem, ba-zman ha-zeh*, "in the past and in the present." What we are saying is that the same God who was present for the Maccabees is the God to whom we turn today. We can debate the particulars of history, but our vitality as a people is found in memory. We are a people of *Zakhor*.

While there is a lot more to say about the book, I do want you to read it, so I will leave it at that. This morning I want to suggest to you that while Yerushalmi's book is a fine piece of scholarship worthy on its own merits, 25-plus years later, on this week of his passing, it reads like a prophetic comment on the Jewish community of today. If I had to diagnose the greatest challenge to contemporary Jewry, I would say it is that our reserves of Jewish memory are running dangerously low. We, who live in an information age, with more knowledge and more access to our past than any other generation, are paradoxically less and less connected to it. We may know history, but when it comes to Jewish memory, our bond with our past has grown increasingly tenuous.

You need look no further than the hero of our Torah reading, Joseph, to understand our present predicament. Joseph's distinction, among others, is that unlike Abraham, Isaac, and Jacob, he is the first Jew who has to create Jewish identity on his own terms, removed from a one-on-one dialogue with God. Without this connection, his vision is skewed entirely in one direction, towards the future. Think about how our *parasha* begins. Joseph is full of dreams, eagerly anticipating his destiny; however, his sense of self is painfully one-dimensional. For Joseph, "any dream will do," but don't call on him to remember. He has absolutely no awareness of his past. There is no indication whatsoever that Joseph knew of his predecessors. It is not so much that Joseph lost his memory; he had no memory to begin with. He is a *tabula rasa*, born with no innate or built-in Jewish content. It is what makes him so intriguing, it is what makes him so reckless, and it is what makes him so relevant for us today.

We are, it would seem, "the Joseph generation," the regrettable fulfillment of Yerushalmi's observations. It would take a sociologist far more learned than I to explain why this rupture or lapse in memory has occurred, but we can observe its effects everywhere. When Israelis define themselves as Israelis first and Jews second, it means that their identities don't extend to Abraham, but only to Ben Gurion or, if we are lucky, Herzl. So too, as many observers of Orthodoxy have noted, the recent shift to the right in Orthodoxy is also attributable to a lack of memory. When one learns how to be Jewish not from parents, but by way of right-wing publications filled with stringent lists of "do's and don't's," it is inevitable that Orthodoxy will become more "by the book," and less open to give and take. The same is true in matters of philanthropy. When the UJA's and JTS's of the world face a diminishing pool of contributors, it means, among other things, that fewer Jews feel an instinctual solidarity and connection with the institutions that have made North American Jewry what it is.

While I can point to the effects of living in "the Joseph generation" around the Jewish world, I see its effects every day here in our community. When our children understand their connection to Israel by way of CNN and not as part of their DNA, then our Zionism is only as strong as the last news-cycle. If we say the words "Never Again" with the Shoah a point of historical reference and not a deeply felt emotional connection, a permanent scar on the Jewish soul, the words risk becoming trite and trivial. The same is true of Jewish observance. We can talk all we want about theology and *mitzvot*, but without memories, theology becomes an empty exercise. Jewish education is more complex than a Rorschach test. You can't flash a text or ritual in front of someone and expect them to respond meaningfully. If we do not give our children points of reference for observance in their *kishkes*, in other words, memories, they are starting from scratch, and to start from the very beginning, *actually*, is a very difficult place to start.

Let me be clear, I am not asking any of us to wax nostalgic about the past. Solomon Schechter once wrote that "every generation must write its own love letters." We can't be satisfied reading those of previous generations. We are not museum curators; we are stakeholders in the Jewish future. What I am asking you to consider is that the most powerful Jewish muscle we have is our Jewish memory. It is our core strength and from it, everything else emerges. As parents and grandparents committed to Jewish education, the most important gift you can give your children is a steady stream of Jewish memories. You light candles at a Friday night table, not as a workshop in theology, but because you are impressing on your children the power of Shabbat. You don't take or send your children to Israel to make them experts in the geopolitics of the Middle East; they need to go now so when they grow up, they will have a reflexive attachment to the land of our people. The child whom you drag to a UJA "phonathon," will not remember years from now, I guarantee, the specifics of the day, but they will remember where your priorities were. When you take your children to *shul* and sit here next to them, it is an investment that will yield dividends for years to come. Our primary educational task in a "Joseph Generation" is to engender a feeling that Jewish commitments begin long before we are born and extend long after we are here on this earth. It sounds strange to say, but it is true: the key to building a Jewish future is the formation of Jewish memory.

Being a dreamer and having memories are not mutually exclusive, in fact they are interdependent. Martin Buber, the most passionate spokesman for Jewish renewal in the 20th century, explained that renewal "must originate in the deeper regions of the people's spirit." As sure as I am that memory without innovation is exhausted nostalgia, I am doubly sure that innovation *without* memory is superficial faddishness. Real Jewish renewal only happens when you are able to turn to the riches of tradition, the accomplishments of the past, and ask the necessary and relevant and pressing questions for this generation and the generations to come. It should not be lost on us that the central pivot, the redemptive turning point of the Joseph story will come next week when Joseph does what he was unable to do in the first half of his life – he remembers: *Vayizkor Yosef et ha-ḥalamot asher ḥalam*, "And Joseph remembered the dreams that he dreamt." (Gen 42:9) The challenge and opportunity of our moment is to be able to do the same, to know that in order to go forward as Jews we must always remember our past. If we want a vital future, we need to understand that the essential task of Jewish education in our schools, *shuls*, and especially in our homes must be the formation of Jewish memory. If we want to dream, then, like Joseph, we must first learn to remember.

Since that walk to *shul* with my daughter, I have often wished that I had given her a slightly amplified answer. I now realize my daughter wasn't seeking history, she was seeking memory. So my answer for my daughter, my answer for the "Joseph Generation," my answer for my congregation, is: "Yes, Moses did walk his children to *shul*, and when we walk to *shul* together, Moses and Abraham and Sarah and Rebecca and even Joseph are *still* walking their children to *shul*. Right here, right now, they are escorting us; and in years to come, when you take your children to *shul*, they will be still be walking right there next to you."

B'shallaḥ
"The Right to Be Different"

President Franklin D. Roosevelt's January 1941 State of the Union address bequeathed to us perhaps the most substantial ideological statement of the Second World War, if not of American rhetoric as a whole. He spoke of the "Four Freedoms," the four essential ingredients of a good society and strong moral order. You may recall them from your high school civics class, or perhaps you heard them spoken by Roosevelt himself: freedom of speech, freedom of religion, freedom from want, and freedom from fear.

What you may not know is that shortly after Roosevelt's address, Simon Rawidowicz, one of the great scholars of modern Jewish thought, penned a famous essay adding one more item to Roosevelt's list. His essay, entitled *Libertas Differendi*, insisted on one more basic freedom that could not be derived from the others: "The Right to be Different," *Libertas Differendi*, the inalienable right of people and groups of people to differ from each other.

While fundamental to America and to all of humanity, this "right to be different" has been part and parcel of Jewish identity more than to that of any other people. Since our infancy, from country to country, through history and time, tolerance and persecution, necessity or choice, it has been our badge of pride that while we inevitably adapt to our surroundings, we have fought valiantly to preserve our inherited state of being different, a "people that dwells alone" in the words of the Torah, in the book of Numbers. Even as we celebrate a common humanity, we believe all groups possess a basic right to be different. Jews, in Rawidowicz's words "the greatest non-conformists in history," have been the strongest advocates for this right throughout our history.

Jewishly speaking, the right to be free is never, as the song goes, merely "to be you and me." The point of freedom is to be "us." A different people, in Hebrew an *Am*, *Goy*, or *Umah*. The thrust of this week's *parasha* is the very gift of freedom, liberty from slavery and the yoke of oppression. Over and over again, it is made abundantly clear that we were not freed merely to enable us to be like others. Freedom was granted in order that we should have the right to be different. Our narrative this week is not so much about the end of slavery as it is about the birth of a people, the formation of *am yisrael*, the nation of Israel. Whether that freedom came at the banks of the Red Sea, the East End of London, Ellis Island, or Galveston, Texas, whenever Jews have arrived safely at the shores of freedom, we have leveraged that very freedom towards writing the next chapter in our people's history.

Our own moment, though it lacks the high drama of the Red Sea or Ellis Island, is yet another pivotal moment of history. Many of you had the honor of hearing John Ruskay's remarks on the occasion of his tenth anniversary as the Chief Executive of UJA-Federation of New York. He explained that today we live at an extraordinary, if not unprecedented, moment in Jewish history. The immigrants of the 20th century have long since arrived; the age of rescue is, more or less, over. We live in a time of a Jewish State, and while Israel's enemies are real and active, Israel today is unquestionably an economic and cultural miracle. In addition, as American Jews, we live, according to Ruskay, "in the most accepting and generous society where Jews have ever lived, having achieved status and influence far beyond what our grandparents could have dreamed." In New York, in Tel Aviv, in Moscow – Jews exist as free men and women on the other side of the sea, removing the mud from our sandals as it were, contemplating what to do with our new-found freedom.

My fear, to put it directly, is that this generation, our generation, has forgotten that, as Jews, the point of our freedom is to be different, to be a unique people. At this moment of unprecedented opportunity, the eternal and internal tug of Jewish peoplehood, I believe, is eroding to dangerously low levels. If I had to diagnose why peoplehood is on the decline, I would attribute it to at least two interrelated forces, coalescing to form a perfect storm.

First, and this has been well documented, is the rise of the sovereign self to the point of a corrosive narcissism. Despite what the polls say, I believe that American Jews are, for the most part, fine with religion, even with Judaism. Most of the Jews I know, a select crowd to be sure, quite like to think of themselves as spiritual and they are willing to let Judaism give expression to their religious needs. But while Jews are willing to achieve their spiritual goals by way of Judaism, they are only willing to do so insofar as it is done on their own terms. There is an inwardness, a privatization, an individualization or, if you like, a my-way-i-fication of what it means to be Jewish. A colleague of mine recently reflected on how as a rabbi he felt akin to being a personal trainer – creating spiritual regimens tailored to each individual. People want *their* occasions marked, *their* loved ones' names announced, *their* Chabad rabbi to study with them over lunch, private tutors for *their* children, *their* philanthropies funded or created. None of these "wants" is necessarily bad, and institutions need to know that Jews, like all consumers, vote with their feet. But an excessive boutiquishness when it comes to Judaism means that Jewish souls are no longer calibrated according to the Jewish calendar - to Pesaḥ, Shavuot, Shabbat, the occasions that make our religion a communal event. Contemporary Jews have lost the ability to subsume the "I" to the "we" and we are all paying the price. Somewhere along the way we have forgotten, in the words of Mordecai Kaplan, that the "self identification of the individual Jew with [his] Jewish People is the source of the mystical element in the Jewish Religion." (*A New Zionism*, p. 114)

The second challenge we face is the excessive universalism of contemporary modes of Jewish expression. When Jews are not looking inward, they are reaching outward beyond what are perceived to be petty parochial concerns towards solving big global problems. Please don't misunderstand what I am saying. We *should* be responsive to the crisis in Haiti; I hope that my words and our synagogue's actions this past week more than make that point. We should and will continue to be concerned with the condition of our shared humanity. But any rabbi knows that it is easier to get a class of high school kids on an alternative spring break to rebuild a church devastated by Katrina than it is to get them to attend their own *shul*. It is easier to get people outraged about the conditions of migrant workers in kosher meatpacking industries than it is to get them to keep kosher. It is easier to get Jews to give to relief efforts in Darfur than to get them to give to the JDC in order to support a Jewish widow living in a walk-up in the FSU, a nice Jewish lady who, were it not for the whims of history, could be any of our mothers or grandmothers. Concern for the non-Jew is important; in fact, it is an expression of core Jewish values. But if all our creative efforts are aimed at the well-being of humanity and none directed at strengthening ourselves, then in a generation or two we will find ourselves without the very community that has given us the very values we are so proud of today.

There are many reasons why peoplehood is on the wane. Our distance from the Shoah; the fact that our Israeli cousins are, for many of us, now second or third cousins; our inwardness; our outwardness – the list goes on. So too the effects of waning peoplehood can be felt everywhere. The lack of dialogue between Jews of different stripes, the weakening of bonds between Diaspora Jewry and Israel, the fiscal and leadership challenges of AJC, WJC, JDC, UJA, ADL or any institution of American Jewish life, synagogues included, whose currency is derived from the coin of "peoplehood." As Ruskay said in the name of Natan Sharansky: "identity is [now] the driver for everything we care about. If one is not positively identified, why care about the Jewish poor, renewing Jewish life in the Former Soviet Union, or securing the Jewish state." Finally, of course, a diminishing sense of peoplehood is directly related to any parent's ability to articulate a counterargument to intermarriage. After all, why on earth should you not marry a wonderful human being of another faith, if the notion of being different, of peoplehood, holds no value for you? Simply put, peoplehood is the lynchpin that holds everything together.

The task of our generation is not to tell our children that they must be Jewish for fear of anti-Semitism – past, present or future – or that they should be Jewish because they owe anyone anything. The argument for leading a Jewish life today is exactly the same as it was thousands of years ago as we stood on the other side of the sea: You have your freedom, earned or inherited, that freedom is yours. *Mazel*

Tov! Now what will you do with it? Will you use your freedom to make you different? Are you able to understand your being part of a grander narrative, a distinct people permeated by past promise and a sense of destiny? Are you willing to be part of the greatest story ever told?

Mordecai Kaplan once quoted the famous mountain climber George Malory, who was asked why he wanted to climb Mount Everest. Malory replied: "Because it is there." So too, Kaplan explained, when asked why be Jewish, we must be able to answer: Because the Jewish people is here, and we are part of it.

We must create engaging, enriching, ennobling, and inspiring Jewish communities. We must give the concept of peoplehood a renaissance, let it regain its religious stature, position it as a compelling point of self-identification for searching Jews. When, and only when, the spiritual wholeness of an individual Jew hangs on being part of a Jewish people and when indifference turns to an embrace of our difference, will our people, the Jewish people, be whole once more.

Yitro
"Remembrance of Torah Past"

Right beneath your nose, just above your upper lip, is something called the *philtrum*. The origins and purpose of that small indentation are, for most of us, a mystery. And while I hope none of us spend much time thinking about our *philtrums* (or to be more precise, *philtra*), you may be interested to learn the rabbinic etiology of the *philtrum*, the Talmudic explanation for how we all received this seemingly functionless facial feature.

According to legend, before we are born, a divine light shining from one end of the universe to the other infuses our souls with wisdom; in fact, the entire Torah is in our possession. At the moment we enter the world, an angel reaches out and raps us on the upper lip, creating the indentation and causing us to forget all our Torah. The hard drive, as it were, is wiped clean. With all of our Torah gone, the rabbis explain that the educational trajectory of our lives is the process of *relearning* the Torah that we actually once knew.

It is a fanciful tale, and probably as strong an explanation as anyone has for this oddity of human anatomy. The question on my mind, however, is what is the point of the story? Apart from demonstrating rabbinic creativity, is there a redeeming lesson to the fable? Perhaps, some say, the purpose of the story is to democratize knowledge, to teach each of us that we are all equally capable of learning Torah; after all, there was a time that each of us possessed it in its entirety. You may have a formal Jewish education, you may not; you may have high or low board scores; you may be rich or poor, young or old. The gift of God's Torah is equally accessible to all. Or, the message could be a bit more cynical, namely, that God believes that there are limits to what human beings should know. While we may have once known the entirety of the Torah, the Almighty, just as in the Garden of Eden, has set boundaries on human knowledge, stop measures if you will, preventing us from knowing too much.

I don't know which answer is right. The rabbis never actually unpack the story. I think, at its most basic level, the point of the *philtrum* story is to explain the nature of Jewish learning. The essential message seems to be that the process of learning in our lifetime, at least Jewishly, is not primarily the act of acquiring new knowledge, but rather reclaiming that which we once knew. Just as the groove above our lip is a part of us, so each of us once possessed the Torah. The learning we do in our lives is a process of remembering – remembering the past, the Torah that was once ours.

Learning happens in all sorts of ways. We learn by experience, inductive learning, deductive learning, acquiring emotional and social intelligence. As the father of four young children, I constantly think about how children learn, what they need to know, how one teaches a child to think. As the rabbi and chief educator of this congregation, I spend quite a bit of time thinking about the necessary canon of Jewish knowledge and how best to impart that body of knowledge to the next generation. I ask myself and the educators around me how we want our children to approach Jewish learning: critically, sympathetically, reverentially, or otherwise. As we re-imagine congregational education and the terms by which it takes place, I wonder if there is a mode of learning sanctioned by the Jewish past and compelling to the Jewish future?

A good starting point is to acknowledge that Jewish learning must be an act of growth and retrieval. Authentic Jewish learning begins with a certain assumption about our hard wiring – that what we learn is not actually constructing new knowledge. We are not a *tabula rasa*; rather, we are engaging with the substratum of our consciousness, or more precisely, with the pre-consciousness of our existence. We move to new ground, and yet return to the familiar.

Look at this week's Torah portion, the giving of the Torah at Mount Sinai. There is an indisputable sense of something new, the bold and thunderous gift of the Torah hitherto unknown to the Jewish people. Yet, there also exists a very rich tradition of Torah that was present before Mount Sinai. After all, how could the Israelites be punished last week for collecting manna on Shabbat, if only this week they receive the law of the Sabbath, the fourth commandment? The laws regarding Passover, the laws regarding circumcision, the obligation to be fruitful and multiply, the reprimand of Cain after Abel's death, the universal laws given following the Flood, and many others – there is a clear legal consciousness prior to Sinai. What is more, the rabbinic tradition imagines the matriarchs and patriarchs to be fully aware of the Torah – studying it, observing it, embodying it – a Torah that predates the events of Mount Sinai. Perhaps most extraordinary are a series of *midrashim*, rabbinic legends, that indicate that the Torah existed even before the world existed, that the Torah was God's blueprint for creation itself.

In this schema, the moment of Sinai is actually an act of retrieval or affirmation, a rejuvenation of an ancient idiom, not the articulation of something totally new. The rabbis do not miss the point that Torah is referred to as the "inheritance of Jacob." (Deut. 33:4) We did not discover or invent Torah, we are merely reclaiming our birthright. The story about the *philtrum* is instructive because it encapsulates the broader message of the biblical narrative itself – namely, that Jewish learning is really a quest to return to our original state of knowledge.

What does this mean in practical terms? It means that every Jewish learning experience should seek both to be a moment of growth and to engender a sense of belonging, familiarity, and return. Many congregants think I am absolutely crazy to go on an Israel trip with young families this summer. After all, why *schlep* all the way there if the kids are too young to really understand the particulars of Israel? I want our parents to take our kids now while they are young because when our kids are older, I want their trip to Israel to be a return to a homeland – the stamp already in their physical and metaphysical passport. As we develop the Congregational School curriculum, I want it to be crafted like an ascending spiral, so that each year when our kids learn about Purim or any holiday, they are both returning to a series of familiar songs, symbols, and stories *and* learning new insights about the festival and about themselves. When you walk into a prayer service, today or any other day, I want you to feel that you are both reaching new heights *and* reconnecting with the substratum of your spirit, that you are hearing melodies both new and familiar. Our Shabbat outreach program is called "Reclaiming Shabbat." I didn't invent the idea of hosting people for Shabbat – I want you to take possession of what is rightfully yours. The list goes on. The problem with Jewish education today is that too often it either possesses an iterative Groundhog Day-like aspect that stifles personal growth, or it is so innovative that it is bears no connection to the roots that actually give it life.

Authentic Jewish learning consists of a lifetime of "aha" moments whereby we arrive at truths about ourselves and our shared humanity, with a sense that those truths have always been there waiting to be discovered. Proust commented in *In Search of Lost Time* that every reader of his novel would recognize in himself what the book says, and that this recognition would be the proof of its veracity. When we learn or do or pray Jewishly, we have succeeded when there is an element of memory and insight, a remembrance of Torah past.

To say it bluntly, this model places a huge educational responsibility on you, the Jewish parent or grandparent. Because while some may believe in angels and *philtra*, I believe in good parenting. You have to take your children to Israel, you have to light Shabbat candles, celebrate the holidays, bring your children to *shul*, talk to them about Jewish identity, provide them with the inheritance that is rightfully theirs. If your children are empty vessels, then they have nothing to return to, nothing to remember, every Jewish experience will be new ground, inauthentic and potentially alienating. I will take care of what happens in this building, but recognize that we are in a partnership. In *your* educational institution – your home and your children's home – I need you to provide the substratum, filling the grooves of young Jewish minds.

In describing the effects of a good book, J.D. Salinger explained, speaking in the voice of Holden Caufield:

> What really knocks me out is a book that, when you're all done reading it, you wish the author that wrote it was a terrific friend of yours and you could call him up on the phone whenever you felt like it.

What is good Jewish education? It is when our children read the Book of Books, the Torah; when they turn to it again and again throughout their lives, both in its newness and familiarity; when after each reading our children wish they could call up its Author – their terrific friend, the Divine giver of Torah, thrilled by new insight and wondering how it is God knew what they were thinking all along. I suspect, in fact I wholeheartedly believe, that at such moments they will feel a divine smile from above, ear to ear, *philtrum* and all.

T'rumah

"Esther, Vashti, and Other Uncomfortable Options for Jewish Women"

When our community gathers next Saturday night for the festival of Purim and the reading of the Scroll of Esther, many of us may feel that we are being offered two objectionable depictions of femininity. The first of the two problematic options appears in the very first chapter: Vashti, queen to the Persian King Achashverosh, refuses to display her beauty before the king and his drunken entourage. While a close reading of the text reveals neither Vashti's reasoning nor exactly how much she was in fact being asked to reveal, we do know that her headstrong refusal resulted in her being banished from the kingdom. God forbid, the king's advisors advise, that Vashti's deeds should go unpunished and wives everywhere exhibit such stubborn disobedience to their husbands. Having asserted her will, Vashti is abruptly cast aside, never again to appear in the narrative, a proto-feminist refusing to be objectified – sacrificing everything, everything that is, except her integrity.

All this is the set-up for the main character, our first Jewish Princess – Esther. At the behest of her Uncle Mordecai, and long before reality TV, Esther enters a beauty contest to compete on "Who Wants to Marry a Monarch?" She is taken into the king's harem, covered in perfume, make-up and finery, a makeover that serves to cover up her most significant feature – her Jewish identity. She wins the competition and is crowned queen, a title that allows her to serve, quite literally, at the pleasure of the King. In fact, her passive demeanor is her dominant characteristic, as she continues to obey the men in her life: Mordecai and her royal husband. Only at the moment of crisis, with the impending threat of Haman's plot, does she take matters into her own hands. Yes, Esther does entrap Haman. Yes, Esther does save the day, but, in doing so, she has betrayed every aspect of her dignity. Awkward questions abound for our Jewish Barbie doll embedded in the Persian seraglio. Can the message really be that for a Biblical woman to impact her people, she may need to give up everything dear to her? At the risk of offending every past, present, and future girl who has dressed up as Queen Esther on Purim... does Esther really embody the values that we want, that *I* want, our daughters to grow up aspiring towards?

Two choices, Vashti and Esther, diametrically opposed and equally unappealing. Many commentators have noted that we are supposed to read the stories of these two figures in light of each other. Vashti refuses to reveal herself and go before the king – a heroic refusal that also leads to her tragic fate. Esther's heroism, by contrast, is found in the very act of doing what Vashti refused to do – appear before the king. What she does do is hide her true self, a posture that comes at a great price. In recent years, a fascinating debate has emerged on these two figures. Which one, if either, shall we take as a role model? Vashti has been elevated to an iconic status in feminist circles for her assertive nature. We should, wrote one author, cheer Vashti's courage just as we do Mordecai's refusal to bow before the king. Recent years have not been kind to Esther, as her formidable achievements have been downgraded – she gave away too much, paid too high a price. She is a hero – but under the cloud of a looming asterisk.

Is this the best our tradition can offer? Are these the only two choices available for women in the ancient world? Are these the only two options contemporary Jewry can offer when it comes to Jewish femininity? Either you are strong-willed and recalcitrant and labeled an uncontrollable shrew, or you can be a submissive, skin-deep beauty queen whose heroism comes by way of pageantry, timely hosting, and temerity. It is an altogether uncomfortable choice that is, unfortunately, not located merely in the past, but in the sexual politics of the present day. Our culture, it would seem, continues to offer women options that are both awkward and undesirable. Must a woman choose between aesthetic grace and ethical fiber? Is there an alternative to a woman besides being labeled either prudish or promiscuous? Does a woman's sense of self come by way of her accomplishments within the household or in the workforce? Can a woman unapologetically embrace every aspect of her womanhood and yet be taken seriously by both men and women?

At every stage of development, women are asked to accept a series of unacceptable choices. Can a liberated woman also possess modesty and restraint or is anything short of Lady Gaga a concession to a man's world? Every week, the news media provide us with reminders of the awkward choices available to women. It is altogether striking to me that in the endless run of prominent men, politicians, and athletes brought down by their marital failings, the husbands are extended the platform to submit fumbling *mea culpas* for their irresponsible and selfish behavior, while their wives are the ones who are presented with the real conundrum. Either stand by your man in all his betrayals and misdeeds, or stand up and walk away. Both decisions have their honor to be sure, but neither one is without its own series of consequences unimaginable to the outside observer.

As the father of three daughters, I think about this issue constantly. What are the choices being extended to my girls? Can a six-year-old avoid being labeled either a "girly girl" or a "tomboy?" What is the role of an overbearing Jewish father in making developmental choices for his daughters while empowering them for the day when they need to make them on their own? How can I communicate to my children the value of health, fitness, diet, and deportment, but protect them from the corrosive images of popular culture that inundate them every minute. This past week, when I went away with my family, I had several hours to ponder the topic as I sat watching each one of my daughters have her hair braided for what seemed to be an interminable amount of time. I sat there with two thoughts in mind. First, I reflected to myself, "Elliot, this is but the first in a lifetime of moments when you will sit quietly as one of your daughters gets her hair done, ears pierced, or whatever the developmental equivalent may be that makes girls, 'girls' or women, 'women' – so get used to the feeling." Second, as I watched my otherwise fidgety kids sit in serene patience anticipating their new 'do', I saw that while I, who grew up in a household of all boys, may not "get it," it was clear as day that for each of them an integrated self-image, both now and in the years ahead, means embracing both the Vashti and Esther of their existence. For them, a choice between assertiveness and docility is a false choice. For them, even at this young age, beauty and brains, backbone and grace are all part of the same package of femininity.

I thought twice about bringing up this topic today. After all, why in the world would I focus on a woman's issue on the day of a young man's *bar mitzvah*, one with two older brothers no less. Statistically speaking, there are far more families of boys here than girls. Besides, apart from being the father of three young girls, I would never think of myself as a hard-charging feminist. But I decided that it is the very realization that this is not "my issue" per se that is actually the point. The task of generating a positive self-image for women is not a woman's issue, it belongs to all of us; we are all stakeholders in the outcome. Each one of us needs to reject the stereotypes so prevalent in the media and commercial culture. As Diane Levin and Jean Kilbourne write in *So Sexy So Soon*, we need to focus on what our children do, not on how they look. We need to provide our daughters with plentiful examples of positive role models that are independent of some idealized image of female perfection. We need to role model for our sons (of which I also have one) the right tone so as not to objectify their female counterparts. Boys and girls need to be provided the cultural cues to grow up embracing their essence while validating their differences. Most importantly, we need to model adult relationships that provide our children, boys and girls, the emotional tools with which to develop deep and meaningful intimate relationships when their time comes. We may be men, we may be women, fathers or mothers, sons or daughters, but it is an issue we all face equally.

So, what does this all mean? Well, in this building it means that when we set policy on what happens in terms of young women wearing *tallis*, *tefillin*, participating in the service, being called *bat kohen*, or whatever the issue of the day may be, the substance of our conversation must be slightly more sophisticated than strident demands either for retaining the received gender roles or for a brute leveling of perceived inequalities. The problem with our tradition is that it is inescapably patriarchal in its formulation, but that is not to say it does not also possess a sense of gender distinction that is worthy of retaining. We need to tread forward very carefully, all the while acknowledging that our real victory is never merely in formulating a policy as to whether a woman can or can't wear *tefillin* or participate in the priestly blessing as a *bat kohen*, but rather to create a culture that acknowledges the different choices that daughters of this congregation may make for themselves. I know that I do not want this congregation to induce the 'damned if you do, damned if you don't' anxiety felt by a woman, mother of four, standing in line at passport control trying to figure out what to fill in on the card that asks you for your occupation. I want this community to be a place where women may wear a *tallis* on a *shabbos* morning or not, but the tone of the room is such that the decision is their own, and everyone else is thinking about their own prayers and not someone else's definition of what makes for an integrated Jewish woman.

There is a tradition, about which you may know, that on Purim one should drink to the point where distinctions are blurred – so much that one cannot tell the difference between black and white divisions, between Mordecai and Haman, the iconic embodiments of good and evil. The message, really the message of Purim as a whole, is that our world is full of problematic lines and polarities. Throughout history and throughout the year, we try to put everything into neat boxes, not just good guys and bad guys, but also good girls and bad girls, Esthers and Vashtis – images of femininity that while good to dress up as for the day, we know deep down are not live options in the long run. Life is not as simple as fairy tales of palace intrigue, and we do our families and community a disservice if we allow our lives to be shaped by paradigms that repress the inherent complexities of our being.

Purim invites us to cross the lines, blur the boundaries, poke fun at ourselves – all with the goal that the next day we should be a little wiser, more humble, and less dogmatic when it comes to the uncomfortable choices imposed on us throughout the year. After all, it is our own skin, not Purim costumes, in which we, our daughters, and our sons, wake up every day of the year. At the very least, at the bare minimum, we should work towards creating a society, congregation, and families filled with people comfortable in our own identities – identities given to each of us by our God in Heaven and ever-present in the Divine spark hidden in each and every one of us.

Va-yak·hel/P'kudei
"Tradition and Change"

Over the past few months, there has been much ado in the press about something called the DSM-V. DSM, short for "Diagnostic and Statistical Manual of Mental Disorders" is also known as "The Psychiatrist's Bible." Every decade or so (we are now on the DSM-V), the American Psychiatric Association (APA) assembles a task force of experts from psychiatry and other related disciplines, for the purpose of drafting a comprehensive register of every psychiatric condition, category, and classification. More than a reference book, this compendium becomes the standard by which all discussions take place in the field of mental health, for instance, what is and isn't a mental disorder, what defines an addiction, is Asperger's syndrome its own condition or on the autism spectrum? The medical, political, legal, and financial implications of the study are huge. Which conditions are or aren't worthy of insurance coverage, who is and isn't eligible for certain services? It also carries significant social implications. Are things like depression, eating disorders, and addictions, often subject to societal disapproval or stigma, actually biological, physiological, or psychological conditions worthy of sympathy and support? The most famous example is the reclassification of Homosexuality in DSM-III. The decision to reclassify homosexuality, previously understood as a treatable disorder, forever changed how the medical and world community approaches matters of human sexuality.

Last week I picked up the phone to speak to the Chair of the DSM-V Task Force, to get into the head of the nation's chief psychiatrist, the chair of the study – Dr. David J. Kupfer. More precisely, he picked up the phone to call me, to check in on how his grandchildren were doing. But in the few minutes I had with my father-in-law before the kids took the phone, we discussed how the study raises some fascinating philosophical questions. How exactly do you rewrite the book about the human condition every ten years? Who has the authority to determine such questions, knowing that the authors of the next study will most likely revise the absolute sureties of present study? Who gets to define what is and isn't a core aspect of the human condition? To use the language of my field, how does one generation define something as *treif* and the next call it kosher and what precisely are the criteria by which these decisions are made?

While I could go on about the DSM study and my father-in-law, the point isn't psychiatry, but rather, the interpretive issues it raises, the process of defining what is and isn't core, what is and isn't kosher and who gets to decide the process and the outcome. A few years ago, Debbie and I were at the San Francisco Museum of Modern Art and we saw Marcel Duchamp's famous work "The Fountain." You may know the story of the piece. It began when Duchamp went to J.L. Iron Works at 118 Fifth Avenue and purchased a standard Bedfordshire model urinal. He went back to his studio, turned the urinal 90 degrees from its normal position, named the piece "the fountain," and entered it into an exhibition. For reasons you can guess, the organizers of the exhibition hid the piece, an inauspicious beginning for a piece of art that was recently voted as the most influential artwork of the 20th century. It is difficult to know when a urinal is a piece of art and when it is… a urinal. It is difficult to know when something is or isn't a psychological disorder.

When it comes to our Judaism, it is equally difficult to determine what is core and what is peripheral to our faith, our practice, and our congregational identity. How do we identify the distinctive and essential features that make us who we are? What practices reflect a sensibility whose time has passed and may actually impede the present and future vitality of our faith? This is without a doubt a very exciting time for our community. It is a time of great strength, but also a time for great reflection and transformation. What is the narrative of Park Avenue Synagogue, what exactly is our distinctive *torah*, how do we define ourselves within our four walls and in the landscape of New York and North American Jewish life? What should our Shabbat morning service look and sound like, how should we conduct our Torah reading? The questions are not only on the ritual front. What is the future of supplementary school education? Are the models that we have received the ones that recommend themselves for the future?

When it comes to making changes, we must always remember that tradition is an incredibly important force; it both stabilizes and anchors our practices in our past. As I have been reading the writings of Milton Steinberg in preparation for his 60th *yahrzeit* next week, I have learned that Steinberg, progressive as he was, was also insistent that modifications in Jewish practice represent "an evolutionary growth rather than a revolutionary break." Change, Steinberg wrote, should not happen just for the sake of change, it should happen when, and only when, it contributes "to the survival of Judaism and... the spiritual self-fulfillment of the individual Jew."

Tradition, we also know, can lead to inertia. More often than not, there is a tendency to glorify the past, to idealize it and therefore become entrenched in it. Like the ark in the wilderness that could not move until the cloud of glory had lifted, the past is often granted an authority that impedes our forward momentum. It is understandable to think that the way things are is the way things must be – we all have an anxiety that change will somehow make us less legitimate than our idealized Jewish past. But this neither is, nor should be, the case.

I'll give you one small example. When I arrived at PAS it was the custom to say an additional *kaddish* at the conclusion of the service following a *dvar torah* by the rabbi. I was struck by the practice because from a gastroenterological perspective it made no sense. Once the service has reached *Ein Keloheinu, Aleinu,* and announcements, all you are thinking about – at least all I am thinking about – is what is being served for *Kiddush.* Why would you teach again at that moment? But I was the new rabbi and I went with it. One day, a long-time congregant explained that at one point in Park Avenue Synagogue history, the congregation felt that each rabbi should speak every Shabbat morning, so a speaking slot was created in addition to the sermon. You may have noticed I have discontinued the practice. It is not that one practice is right and one is wrong; the point is that it was a custom that arose under certain circumstances, circumstances that are no longer applicable.

There is a difference between the past serving as a steadying force in our congregational mission and the past serving as a filibuster that undercuts our ongoing vitality and efforts towards renewal. There are some, wrote Steinberg's teacher Mordecai Kaplan, who "will always assume a deprecatory attitude toward [change]… on the ground that the Jewish religion would attain a form that its Jewish forebears would not recognize." The error in this approach," wrote Kaplan, "is that it proceeds from the assumption that those who are to determine whether or not the continuity of a culture is maintained are its founders or initiators, and not its spokesmen in the generations following." "The only ones," concludes Kaplan, "to decide whether the continuity of a culture is maintained are those who are actually confronted with the problem. The past or its proxies can no more pass judgment upon the present than the child can sit in judgment upon the man." (*Judaism as a Civilization*, p. 404)

There is nothing I take more seriously than being entrusted to shape the identity, practices, programs, and schools of this congregation. I am constantly thinking about where we have come from, our desired results, and the process by which we will create a shared vision and achieve our goals, whether we are considering what our Shabbat morning service looks like or how the congregational school is structured. While this conversation is only beginning, let me share with you three preliminary ground rules for our journey forward. Number 1: Our conversations cannot begin with the bludgeoning statement, "This is the way we have always done it." The beauty of this congregation is that the more I learn about it, the more I discover that there are very few things that "have always been done" a certain way. Besides, it is our commitment to our congregation's unrealized future, not a loyalty to an idealized past, that must determine our present needs.

Secondly, conversations that take place under my watch will not be framed in a black and white, either/or fashion: we will either have a 2-day- or a 3-day-a-week Hebrew School; we will either have a full or a triennial Torah reading. I am dogmatic that we are not dogmatic. Such formulations are not only unhelpful, but they are divisive and, worst of all, demonstrate an abject lack of creativity. The questions that I want answered are what are the spiritual and intellectual needs of the Jews in this sanctuary and those Jews *potentially* in this sanctuary? I want to ask: What is the most compelling model of congregational education for a community as diverse as ours, for a community that exists in a city with a myriad of other educational choices? One day we will inevitably have to make certain choices, but I have a hunch that if we are as good as I think we are, when that day comes, the answers will be self-evident.

Thirdly and finally, it is my job – our job – to formulate an explicit or implicit narrative of what our community stands for, a *torah* of Park Avenue Synagogue, if you will, different from any other congregation in the city, different from the Park Avenue of ten years ago and different from the Park Avenue of ten years from now. Whether we are psychiatrists, art critics, or committed Jews, our mandate is to assess the moment in which we find ourselves, to sort through the available options, and formulate the most thoughtful and passionate response that we are capable of creating.

Ultimately, I don't know, and none of us know, if what we are doing will be judged kosher or *treif* by the generations to come. What I do know is that I want people to look back at these years and say that the lay and professional leadership left it all out on the field working tirelessly to serve God and the Jewish people. I hope that future generations appreciate our present efforts and I pray they will be smart enough to know that when it is their turn, they need to come up with the answers right for their age, not ours.

There is a story in the Talmud (B. Menachot 29b) that as Moses goes up to Heaven, as an act of comfort, God allows Moses see the future legacy of the Torah first given at Mt. Sinai. God transports Moses to visit the academy of Rabbi Akiva, the great rabbinic sage who lived some 1400 years after Moses. Moses sits in the back row of Akiva's classroom, and not surprisingly, does not understand a single thing Akiva is teaching, never mind agreeing or disagreeing with him. He is thoroughly disoriented and discomfited by the experience. But then Moses hears that in response to a student's question, Akiva cites that such and such law was given to Moses at Sinai. At that point Moses is comforted, realizing that his Torah takes on new forms in new settings, that there is an ongoing coherence even though the content may be unfamiliar to him.

May we, as creative and committed Jews have done throughout history, continue to formulate a Judaism responsive to the Jews of *our* time, foreign and familiar both to those who came before and to those future generations who will come after.

Va-yikra

"Prisoner of Hope: 60th *Yahrzeit* of Rabbi Milton Steinberg, z"l"

It is my distinct honor and privilege to offer a sermon in memory of Rabbi Milton Steinberg on the occasion of his 60th *Yahrzeit*. On behalf of the entire congregation, I want to welcome Rabbi Steinberg's sons, Dr. David Steinberg and Dr. Jonathan Steinberg, and their family and friends who have gathered from near and far. We look forward to hearing your words immediately following *Kiddush*. From your presence at my installation, to the friendship you have shown me every step of the way as we have conceived and planned this weekend, please know how grateful I am for your counsel, support, and encouragement as I take my own steps in the extended shadow of your father's pulpit.

The honor of speaking today, great as it is, also comes with its share of anxieties. To what aspect of Rabbi Steinberg's rabbinate shall we direct our attention? His congregational achievements, his theology, his fiction, or perhaps his book that will be posthumously released tomorrow? For a brief time, I thought I should just deliver one of his published sermons, so that the gathered family could experience his words spoken by my humble proxy. It is an impossible task to encapsulate the totality of Rabbi Steinberg's rabbinate; the combination of Steinberg's interpersonal skills, felicitous pen, and leadership qualities left a profile encompassing a trusted pastoral presence, a community builder, as well as a leader in Jewish institutional, literary, and ecumenical life.

Given the options, I will begin where he did just over sixty years ago, with a sermon on Passover, by way of notes preserved by Bernard Mandelbaum. The sermon is about suffering and it bears the title "Rabbi Levi's Prayer." In his sermon, Steinberg cites another sermon, given by Rabbi Levi Yitzhak of Berdichev, the saintly figure of 18th-century Hasidism. Rabbi Levi Yitzhak introduces the subject of human pain and suffering by way of the famous passage in the Passover Haggadah on the four sons:

> "The Haggadah speaks of four sons," Rabbi Levi explains, "One wise, one wicked, one simple, and one who does not know how to ask. Lord of the world, I, Levi Yitzhak, am the one who does not know how to ask. Lord of the universe, even if I did know, I would not dare to. How could I venture to ask You why everything happens as it does, why we suffer, why we are driven from one exile to another, why our foes are allowed to torment us?" Rabbi Levi continued in his cry to God, "But the Haggadah explains to the father of this fourth child: The father must take the initiative. Lord of the world, are You not my Father? Am I not Your son? I do not even know what questions to ask. I do not beg You to reveal to me the secret of your ways – I couldn't comprehend it! But please show me one thing. Show me the meaning of what is happening to me at this moment. Show me what it demands of me. Show me what You, Lord of the universe, are telling me through it. I do not ask why I suffer. I ask only to know that I suffer for your sake.

It is a terse and enigmatic homily, a message preached by Rabbi Levi Yitzhak in Berdichev some two-and-a-half centuries ago in the midst of torment, and a message preached by Rabbi Steinberg on the Upper East Side in the late 1940's. The earnest fourth child, in possession of a question he dare not ask, "I do not ask why I suffer. I ask to know only that I suffer for your sake." It is both a remarkable concession and an insistent demand. He knows the inevitability of pain, he knows the life of quiet desperation that most men lead; he accepts pain as an unwelcome but necessary part of the human experience. But what Levi Yitzhak wanted to know, what Milton Steinberg wanted to know, what every human being who has experienced or witnessed pain wants to know is "For what purpose is this suffering?" In secular terms: "Is there something good to come of it?"

Steinberg's intellectual legacy cannot be summed up neatly. In his far too brief life, his oeuvre touched on the full range of Jewish study and concern. But in those final few years, when this sermon was written, at the peak of his intellectual prowess, as he crafted and drafted the novel that will be released tomorrow, he stood face to face with what his student, and product of this congregation, Arthur Cohen, called, "the Tremendum." The overwhelming theological questions raised by standing in relationship with a God under whose watch the Holocaust took place. Steinberg could not stand on the sidelines. Given his national profile, he was asked to speak again and again, to mobilize American Jewry, to provide relief to refugees, to raise funds on their behalf, to build up the fledgling state of Israel, and most difficult of all, to make sense of the Shoah to a Jewry in search of meaning. His addresses, published and unpublished, on behalf of agencies such as the JDC, the National Jewish Welfare Board, the National Refugee service, bear titles such as "That These Dead Shall Not Have Died in Vain: Four Messages from the Dead – Addressed to Us, The Living," "Breathe Upon these Slain and They Shall Live."

Perhaps Rabbi Steinberg's most heart-searing address was delivered at the Waldorf Astoria to the Women's Division of the United Jewish Appeal in 1944. In it, he speaks of Seraye, "a village situated in the Lithuanian County of Suwalki, just to the east of the old German frontier." A village, in Steinberg's words "whence my family stems, where my father was born." Listen to his words: "I say that I have been thinking about Seraye a great deal of late [because] I cannot think about all of Europe's Jews, the six million dead, the one and a half million of walking skeletons. Such numbers are too large for me to embrace, the anguish they represent are too vast for my comprehension. And so I think of Seraye instead." Steinberg recounts imagined people and scenes of this village that is no longer, the countless Serayes destroyed by the Nazis. He is filled with anguish and anger, "Sometimes," he writes, "when I think of Seraye, I want to hurl hard words at God, that terrible saying of Abraham; 'Shall the Judge of the whole earth not do Justice?!'"

If the first part of Steinberg's life was devoted to negotiating the dialectic between faith and reason, secularism and piety, universalism and particularism, then I believe the last few years of Steinberg's life were devoted to the question of suffering – national, personal, and otherwise. From his public addresses and his sermons to his study of 19th-century European philosophers (especially Kierkegaard), Steinberg's questions turned again and again to the question of human suffering, the Divine and the human response to our agonies. It would be during these years that Steinberg would come to say "I still revere a great mind, but I revere a great heart more. In part because, like everyone else in our generation, I have discovered of what monstrosities the merciless intellect is capable."

There is a deeply human and sometimes plaintive quality to his writing in the final years of his life: The following is from his 1947 Yom Kippur sermon, "A Pity for the Living": "The hard tragic fact is that of the universality of suffering, the truth that to live is to suffer... All life is a great fellowship of anguish in which each of us participates in some fashion or other." Steinberg concludes "that because all things suffer, things merit our pity." One human being to another, or a God to a suffering humanity, our agony must not be for naught, it must, as Rabbi Levi Yitzhak said, lead to a deepening of the human spirit.

Sixty-plus years later it is difficult to connect all the dots. I cannot say with absolute surety if Rabbi Steinberg was drawn to the question of suffering solely because of the Shoah. That was probably part of it, but probably so was his heart condition and his deteriorating health due to his frenetic schedule. Or it could simply have reflected maturity of thought, that after shuttling between faith and reason, secular philosophy and devotional learning for decades, he decided to slice it another way – directing his energies inwards, directly towards the human condition. Certainly, as a rabbi, one has many opportunities, plenty of late nights in hospital rooms at the side of congregants standing face-to-face with the question of "For what purpose is this suffering?" Steinberg's theological legacy is important not only because of his philosophical rigor, but because his writing was wrought by way of a deep engagement with a suffering humanity.

Steinberg did not live long enough to write a systematic exposition of his own religious thinking, and, as we know, he died before he completed his novel. But if granted length of years, he, like Rabbi

Levi Yitzhak would know what every human being comes to know: that while it is not for us to escape suffering, and it is not for us to understand it completely, it is in our capacity to determine how we bear it and how purposefully we lead our lives. "If his suffering turns him in on himself," wrote Steinberg, "makes him cruel, selfish, bitter, then will he think ill not only of himself, but of the whole human species and God. If on the other hand his pain renders him merciful, if he carries it off with dignity, then he has given himself a demonstration of man's nobility."

There are questions about which we cannot ask and to which we will never have answers, but each of us can, every day of our lives, respond with gentleness, compassion, pity, and concern. Even in the face of suffering, we can come to appreciate God's world. In fact, I would venture to say that Steinberg's able pen and supple heart would have found a way to express that it is the very vulnerability of our lives that can draw us into this greater appreciation. He hints at that very thought in what is understood to be his finest sermon, "To Hold with Open Arms." It is a meditation upon leaving the hospital after a massive heart attack. He steps out of the hospital, awed by the eminently ordinary – the sunlight, breeze, and humanity ignored by a healthy humanity. In the very recognition of life's fragility, we can embrace our world and our God with open arms.

Rabbi Steinberg knew the brittle shell of our common humanity. The rabbis employ the image of vessels in a potter's shop, tapped by the hammer of our Divine maker to check for quality – and yes, sometimes tapped so hard that we shatter. For Steinberg, this condition did not yield to gloom and cynicism. Prisoners we are, but for Steinberg we are prisoners of hope. To paraphrase his final address, above our suffering, beyond our doubts, and aside from the questions we dare not ask, lies something else – hope. Hope for humanity, hope for each of us, and hope for a world in need of redemption. May this message, some sixty years later, bring with it comfort and uplift in our day as it did in the time of Rabbi Steinberg, and may the memory of Rabbi Milton Steinberg, *Harav Micha'el ben Shmuel Halevi*, be for a blessing and enduring legacy for generations to come.

Sunday, March 21, 2010

Book Launch: Rabbi Milton Steinberg's The Prophet's Wife

If it were the case that Rabbi Milton Steinberg, z"l, had only led this congregation from 1933 until his untimely death in 1950, building it from a sleepy Depression-era congregation to a beacon of intellectual, social, and religious activity in American life – that would have been enough. We would, as did my distinguished predecessor Rabbi David Lincoln ten years ago at Steinberg's 50th *yahrzeit*, convene our community to reflect on his legacy.

If seventy years since the publication of *As A Driven Leaf*, we were to have a conversation on the impact of Rabbi Steinberg's most famous novel, to debate the question of the contemporary literary appropriation of sacred texts, and to ponder the continued reception this book has had on its readers, that too – *dayenu* – would have been enough. If we were to have discovered, as we did, a manuscript of Steinberg's unpublished novel, *The Prophet's Wife*, and wanted to release it to the public from Rabbi Steinberg's pulpit – *dayenu* – without a doubt, that would have been enough. Moreover, if we wanted to have a dialogue about the forces that gave rise to Steinberg's intellectual profile, and ask the question of the ongoing relevance of the questions he raised for contemporary Jewry, and bring together the brightest lights of national Jewish life to do so, I am sure – *dayenu* – that too would be enough.

How extraordinary it is that this afternoon we are able to remember our congregational leader, to reflect on his literary legacy, to release his hitherto unseen novel, and to bring together a distinguished panel to discuss Rabbi Milton Steinberg in his historical context and raise the question of his enduring legacy. I want to thank the leadership of Park Avenue Synagogue, our chairman Steven M. Friedman, David Behrman of Behrman House Publishing, and Gary Rosenblatt of *The Jewish Week* for the collaborative spirit and hard work that enabled us to arrive at this literary event. Thank you to our special events lay committee led by Jean Bloch Rosensaft and to Carolyn Hessel of the Jewish Book Council; our professionals, Rabbi Julia Andelman and Marga Hirsch, and the entire PAS staff, who have worked tirelessly to make today what it is; the Behrman House team, including Dena Neusner and Jessica Gurtman, who have worked very hard; and of course, Beth Lieberman, who took a raw manuscript and rendered *The Prophet's Wife* a publishable work.

Most of all, I want to acknowledge the presence of Rabbi Steinberg's sons Dr. Jonathan Steinberg and Dr. David Steinberg and their gathered family and friends, who have extended friendship and counsel as this weekend was being planned. I am personally grateful to you for your support as I take my own steps in the long shadow of your father's pulpit. Finally, while it is for our distinguished moderator Gary Rosenblatt to introduce our panelists, I do want to offer my deepest gratitude to Rabbi Dan Ehrenkrantz, Dr. Arnold Eisen, Dr. Adriane Leveen and Rabbi Dr. Jacob J. Schachter for your participation today, and of course to our keynote speaker, Rabbi Dr. Harold Kushner, who along with Ari Goldman and Norma Rosen, wrote prefatory essays to *The Prophet's Wife* and shepherded the project to completion. To Rabbi Kushner and everyone involved in the publication of *The Prophet's Wife*, I do hope that today serves as an expression of the blessing of the psalmist, "You shall enjoy the fruit of your labors; and you shall be happy and you shall prosper." (Psalm 128)

I believe that at least part of the reason behind Milton Steinberg's enduring legacy lies in the fact that his profile straddled a multitude of influences and interests. He was a pulpit rabbi, first in Indianapolis and then here at Park Avenue Synagogue. He held a national profile, speaking to and on behalf of North American Jewry, especially during and immediately following the Shoah, mobilizing his audience to provide relief to the refugees, to raise funds on their behalf, and to build up a fledgling State of Israel. He was a scholar, a product of a unique and cerebral moment of American Jewish history, a student at City College when it was largely composed of children of Jewish immigrant parents. Under the influence of Morris Raphael Cohen, Steinberg embodied a lifelong dialogue between Jewish sources and secular philosophy, right up until his final address months before his death. Never limited to the ivory tower, Steinberg was, and is, a popular literary figure whose books, especially *As A Driven Leaf* and *Basic Judaism*, continue to be the books most recommended by pulpit rabbis across the country.

Finally, Steinberg represents a fascinating snapshot of denominational identity. He transcends simple categorization. He was often referred to as Mordecai Kaplan's pre-eminent disciple and spokesman for Reconstructionist Judaism (a Paul, if you will, to Kaplan's Jesus). But as provocative discussions this weekend have revealed, these labels are somewhat facile and worthy of further exploration. Even the manner by which Steinberg got the job here at Park Avenue Synagogue reveals the inadequacy of denominational labels. As Laurie Harris explains in her article on Steinberg's arrival at Park Avenue Synagogue in the PAS 125th anniversary volume, in 1933 Park Avenue Synagogue was a Reform temple in need of a new rabbi. The executive secretary, Manny Rosenthal, was instructed to take a Fifth Avenue bus to the seminary and find a rabbi. At the time, Fifth Avenue was two-way, and Rosenthal got on an uptown bus instead of one that went downtown to the Reform rabbinical seminary. When he asked the driver to let him off at the rabbinical school, the driver had him get off at 122nd Street, at the Jewish Theological Seminary. He got off the bus, and went to the office of Dr. Finkelstein, who realized Rosenthal was in the wrong place, but wasn't going to miss the opportunity. He sent Steinberg to interview, Steinberg got the job, and, to make a long story short, Park Avenue Synagogue is now the flagship synagogue not of HUC-JIR, not of RRC, but of JTS. As for Orthodoxy, it is for good reason that I welcome Rabbi Dr. Schachter from YU. As correspondence I have saved from my own grandfather – an Orthodox rabbi in dialogue with Dr. Kaplan – reveals, there was a time when the question of the degree to which Reconstructionist Judaism represented a movement on its own, or merely an inflection of an existent denomination, was a *very* open point of discussion.

Ultimately, the book release of Steinberg's unfinished novel serves as a ready metaphor for today's symposium. Steinberg died before completing this book, and he also did not live long enough to write a systematic exposition of his own religious thinking. As with Puccini who died before finishing his *Turandot*, we do not know how he would have finished if given the opportunity. Beyond the unspeakable personal loss to the Steinberg family, the tragedy of Steinberg's premature death is that if granted length of years, I believe that in addition to his completed work, his subsequent novels and theology would sit alongside every other post-Holocaust theologian from Heschel, Buber, and Jacobs to A.J. Wolf, Berkovitz, Soloveitchik, and beyond. The depth and range of Steinberg's knowledge reflect an inimitable set of historical circumstances that would be difficult, if not impossible, to replicate. Any examination of Rabbi Steinberg's legacy, today included, bears this lingering "what if."

Yet, while the sea does not overflow, fortunately, the springs remain. In fact, on a day like today, I would call Steinberg's enduring legacy a *ma'ayan mitgaberet*, a wellspring that grows stronger each day – instructive, if not required, reading for those wishing to participate in future discussions of constructive Jewish theology. The tensions that were crystallized in him, though still resonating throughout American Jewry, are on some level representative of a bygone era. Nevertheless, the forthright, clear, honest, and synthetic manner in which he conducted his quest – connected with the past, at home in traditional literature, in sympathy with humanity – remains a model that transcends the limitations of his life and the world that produced him.

May the memory of Rabbi Milton Steinberg, *Harav Micha'el ben Shmuel Ha-levi*, be for a blessing. I thank you for being here and for ensuring this discussion continues into the years ahead.

Passover, First Day
"Staying Power"

"Style... ain't nothing but keeping the same idea from beginning to end." So said the great Pulitzer Prize-winning Pittsburgh playwright August Wilson. It is within our capacity to see and sustain a thought, from its origins into unseen future horizons; that is the measure of who we are. If this is the litmus test we have set, both in terms of style and substance, then our world, our society – we ourselves – fall altogether short.

We live in an age of diminished staying power, a time of short, intense, and fleeting bursts of information. We click on and click off world events at a dizzying pace. The top news stories are no longer the ones that actually matter; rather, they are the ones that are most emailed from one co-worker to another. In this world the sex scandal of a professional athlete can derail relief efforts in the third world, the passage of legislation of generational import is contingent on our ability to shoehorn it into our attention span. Darfur, Haiti, Katrina, Tsunamis – who remembers any of these anymore? Our world, flattened by technology, has taken on a Teflon quality. An issue emerges, it eclipses everything, we lose sight of everything else and then it is gone like the wind. It is not a matter of setting a hierarchy because every moment and every crisis is important. What has changed is the manner by which we receive, process, and then dismiss the events of our lives. We have become consumers of instant information, instant response, snap judgments, and fast dismissal. As a culture, we have – to use Wilson's term – no "style."

You may recall Malcolm Gladwell's book *Blink*. It's a great book and a quick read, which is appropriate, because it is all about rapid cognition. The book is about the kind of thinking that happens in the blink of an eye; Gladwell calls it "thinslicing." He explains that when you meet someone for the first time, or walk into a house you are thinking of buying, or read the first few sentences of a book, your mind takes about two seconds to jump to a series of conclusions. *Blink* is a book about those two seconds, the powerful and instant conclusions that we reach, sometimes spot on and sometimes off-base, with horrific consequences. For example, Gladwell describes an experiment where a psychologist gave college students three 10-second soundless videotapes of a professor lecturing. The students were then asked to rate that professor. Their ratings matched the ratings from students who had taken the professor's course for an entire semester. On the other hand, the powers of rapid cognition can have ghastly consequences. In a chapter called "Seven Seconds in the Bronx," Gladwell describes the horrendous series of snap judgments made by the New York City police officers who shot and killed Amadou Diallo. From love at first sight to racial profiling, our minds are calibrated to a point where judgments are collapsed into a hairbreadth of space. Gladwell explains that "we need to accept the mysterious nature of our snap judgments. We need to respect the fact that it is possible to know without knowing why we know and accept that – sometimes – we're better off that way." (*Blink*, p.52)

Gladwell may be right. I am no neurobiologist, so I can hardly speak to the science of human cognition. It may indeed be human nature to be able to process a million bits of information in an instant. It may be the case that the outward pace by which society moves is merely a reflection of our internal human abilities. But I have to believe that whether or not it is intrinsic to the nature of humanity, it is decidedly not the nature of being Jewish. It is not an indication of maturity, and it is certainly not the nature of our task on Passover. If there is one message of today, one lesson to be learned, it is that as important as the present moment may be, for us as Jews it must be couched between past and future. Passover insists that we never lose sight of the broader context, the grand arc in which we function and exist. Put simply, Passover is the "Anti-Blink holiday." It is a day which acknowledges that it may indeed be human to thinslice, it may be who we are to work and react on impulse, but it is not who we should aspire to be – it is not what being Jewish is all about.

Think about the Haggadah that we read last night and that we will read again this evening. The power of the *seder* is found in two deeply embedded operating principles. First of all, and I encourage you to think about this tonight, the Exodus from Egypt is never read merely as an isolated moment. The Exodus is the fulfillment of a promise made long before the redemption from Egypt. *Barukh shomer havtahato l'yisrael*, "Blessed be the One who keeps His promise to Israel," a promise made to Abraham, to Isaac, and Jacob, that sustained our forefathers in their bondage. Secondly, the redemptive message of Exodus is never limited to that single historical event, but serves as a standing promise and recurring opportunity for every generation. In every generation, when we sit at the seder table, we are asked to enter a mystical temporal matrix whereby we are both recalling an ancient past and anticipating a redeemed future at the same time. Every year we begin by remembering our slavery, every year we end by promising "Next year in Jerusalem." Every year we recall our wandering ancestor, every year we tell of our rise to freedom. If you stop to think about it, the whole business is incredibly countercultural. It doesn't matter what is going on in the news, how the markets are doing, what Oprah's book of the month is, or whether Tiger Woods is or isn't making a comeback. The whole point seems to be that the story you told last night is the same story you are going to tell tonight, and exactly the same one that you told last year, the one that was told to you when you were a child, that was shared generations ago, and that will, please God, be told in generations to come. The story is relevant not because it changes with the times, it is ever relevant because it is a story that exists in the substratum of our souls and speaks to us year after year, no matter where we are.

Our age is deficient in terms of stamina of vision, we lack an enduring attention span. We treat everything like a stock that is bought and sold, forgetting that identity occurs over the long term. There is nothing wrong with being attentive and responsive, it can be altogether commendable, but there are consequences to living solely in the instant. When you live solely in the moment, the relationships that mean the most to you can be obscured through lack of perspective. Be it a sibling, a spouse, or Israel, to lack perspective means that the totality of a relationship can be eclipsed by any single news cycle.

To live solely in the moment means that every scene of our lives is of equal weight, that the promises and commitments of the past are effortlessly and carelessly trumped by our fickle hearts and minds.

The Passover Haggadah is significant, not only because of its content, but because it teaches us how to be Jews, it teaches us how to be human beings. We, like God, seek to keep our promises through thick and thin. We, like ancient Israel, seek to persevere and hold tight to our principles even when they are inconvenient or appear passé. Passover reminds us that we are part of a bigger story, a story that began long before any of us and will continue long after. We remember where we came from, we stand committed to our destiny, and that gives balance to our present. We never allow the isolated moment to dominate because who we are is so rooted in our past and our future.

Menachem Mendel of Lubavitch once described the natural spiritual posture of a Jew as existing in *Hoveh tamid*, "the Eternal Present." More than any other people, as Jews we are taught that the intense "nowness" of our present is always linked both to our past and to our future. In a very different context, Paul Ricoeur, the late great philosopher of the University of Chicago, observed that the Jewish conception of time has no sense of an "isolated punctual instant," rather the present is "always directed toward the past though memory and toward the future through expectation." If I were to rephrase Ricoeur in Wilson's language, I would say: "Being Jewish ain't nothing but keeping the same idea from beginning to end." If I were to rephrase Ricoeur and Wilson in Jewish coin, I would quote the Haggadah, *Lo et avoteinu bilvad ga'al ha-kadosh barukh hu, eleh af otanu ga'al imahem,* "Not only our forefathers alone did the Holy One redeem, but He redeemed us too with them." This year, let us see our families, ourselves, and our lives for what they are, part of the grandest story of all – ever present, ever past and ever future – the eternal present of our Jewish existence.

Passover, Eighth Day:
"The Four Children... of Grief and Recovery"

In every generation, at every Passover *seder*, we return to the iconic passage of the four children. Four children: wise, wicked, simple, and the one who does not know how to ask. In every reading, we know that these children represent far more than first appears, and have been interpreted differently throughout the ages. Some interpretations draw on educational theory – that the four represent four Jewish approaches to learning: a posture of submission (the wise child), of criticism (the wicked), simplicity, and ignorance. Rabbi Yoseph Schneerson once explained that the four children represent four generations of the American experience: the wise child with roots in the European *shtetl*; the wicked child brought up in the American melting pot – cynical to his parents' generation; the next generation, confused by his grandfather's reverence and father's irreverence, and then the fourth generation who, as a consequence of his mixed-up pedigree, has woken up not even able to formulate a question. Israeli Haggadot have similarly adopted the template of the four children with respect to attitudes towards the Zionist dream; women's Haggadot have used the iconography of these children to portray the changing face of feminism. A simple passage, but not so simple – one that continues to resonate to different effect year in and year out.

This morning, as we arrive at *Yizkor*, reflecting on the absence of our loved ones and the storehouse of memories that we are about to open, I want to draw on the image of the four children one last time during this festival. Not as a meditation on assimilation or feminism, but on the process of loss and recovery, how a person receives the blow of the death of a loved one, and then journeys forward. I want to share with you a modern *midrash* if you will, as to how the four children represent the manner by which we may reconstitute our own lives in the face of grief, as we walk through our own valleys in the shadow of death.

We work backwards from the fourth child, the one who cannot speak. When death occurs, this is the first step. The punch to the stomach, the gasp for air, the realization that our father, our child, our brother or sister or life partner has died. There is a numbness. As in Edvard Munch's famous painting "The Scream," we open up our mouths, but nothing comes out. At the moment when Aaron received the news of the death of his sons, he did not cry, yell, or scream, he was silent: *Vayidom Aharon*. The tradition notes the similarity between *Vayidom* and the Hebrew word for blood, *dam*, explaining that upon hearing of their death, it was as if the blood was drawn from him. He was cut loose from his moorings, hit by a tidal wave of despair. So many questions. Why? How could such a thing come to pass? Why not me? According to Jewish law, you do not become a mourner, an *avel*, until after burial, only then do you say *kaddish*. The period from the news of death until burial is called *aninut*. Catapulted into death, you cannot be consoled, grief is inexpressible – comfort or healing is altogether premature. This is the one who cannot speak. This is the bottom rung from which we must climb.

And climb we do, because however painful, whether death happens suddenly or after prolonged illness, all of us know, on some level, that we are mortal. Even as we rend our garments, feeling that which is dearest to us being torn away, we know that there is a simple truth, the third child, embedded somewhere in our collective consciousness. From dust we come and to dust we go. Everyone has a limited number of years on this earth. We realize that we are not the first to have lost a parent. There is another who has felt this pain – mourning after all is one of the very few experiences shared by all of humanity. So we allow for a hug, we allow for a kind word, we are brittle, but we are willing to let ourselves be touched by our family, by our community, for in that contact comes the restorative reminder that we are still alive. It is actually Jewish law that when you return from the cemetery you must eat a meal. Why? Because it reminds us that we are still alive. We are not yet ready to move on, we hurt, but we must recognize that it is not we who have died. Our questions are simple, fumbling inklings that we are aware of our world. *Mah zot?* What is this? What is this world that we have woken up to – as a widow, as an orphan? There are questions to which we know we will never receive full answers, but at least here and now, in this stage, we are able to find our voice, to shed tears, tears that may just plant the seeds for fruit to be reaped another day.

As anyone who has grieved will tell you, however, just as there are steps forward, there are steps backward. As Elizabeth Kübler Ross explained in her book *On Death and Dying*, there will be a time for anger, resentment, and depression. The second child comes in all forms, but it all reflects the same impulse – a refusal to accept this narrative as your own. This is not the story as it should have happened; it wasn't supposed to be this way. We say: "The physicians didn't do enough. Maybe I didn't do enough. The rabbi wasn't there when I needed him. My loved one didn't hold on long enough. Where are my friends now? Where did everyone go after *shiva* ended? How dare people plan their future when I can't see the next day? The resentment of the second child is not good or bad, wicked or otherwise, it is just resentment, pure and simple. We are frustrated, we are alone, we are in pain, we are alienated from everyone who doesn't know our hurt and we are angry. As the poet wrote: "We read the world wrong and say that it deceives us." (Tagore, *Stray Birds*, LXXV) We are the second child.

The stage of the second child may last for a long time or for a little. Our constitutions are inherently different, loss follows no set recipe. Each of us proceeds at his or her own pace. But we know, here on Yizkor, that we aspire to be the wise first child, with the possibility of acceptance, the child of hope. *Haḥam*, "wise" is a carefully chosen word. Nothing is whitewashed, our grief remains, but somewhere along the way we have chosen to leverage our loss towards understanding and growth, towards asking the questions that we couldn't ask upon the news of death, that can't be asked simply, that we rejected in our anger. Now we know that we must learn to reflect on legacy, to think back and consider how the values, qualities, and high ideals of our loved ones transcend death and how they inform our lives. We wonder how we are shaped by them, as an extension of and reaction to the generations that came before. It is not for any of us to change the past; our relationships with our loved ones had their strengths and weaknesses. But we the living have been entrusted and empowered to craft and draft our own narratives of memory, to tell the story to ourselves and to those around us – after all, it is Passover. The wise child knows that given the fragility of life, the acute awareness of our mortality wrought by the loss of those we love, we here in this room must live lives worthy of remembrance. The stage of wisdom is hopefully not so much any one stage or destination, but rather a philosophy of existence reflecting resignation and acceptance, anchors of memory and breezes of hope all mixed together.

Anyone who has studied the Haggadah knows that ultimately, the most important thing to say about the four children is not about one or the other, but about the four of them together. They are not necessarily discrete individuals; rather they are four aspects of all of our beings. Each one of us has elements of the four. The point, we know, is that no matter how wise, how wicked, how simple, or how introverted, each one has a place at the table, and they are all seated at the *seder*.

It would seem that what is true for the *seder* table, is true for this moment of *Yizkor*. We who are gathered here recognize the continuum of grief. On any given day we may find ourselves to be at one stage or another. But when we say *Yizkor*, every emotion is present and accounted for. We are at a loss being reminded of the death of our loved one; we grieve in the context of a community, finding comfort in the knowledge that we are not alone; we resent, as is our right, our losses; and we are not afraid to bring that emotion into this sanctuary. We also seek wisdom – to draw from the well of memory in hope that it provides sustenance for the years ahead.

One final thought – perhaps unexpected but also a bit inevitable. Maybe, just maybe, the point of the four children is not the children themselves, their qualities, and what they represent. Maybe the point is the one thing, or better yet, the one person, that all of them have in common – the parent who greets them all at the *seder* table. I have often thought that the real lesson of this passage is to reflect on the role of the parent, that divine personality, who created a *seder* table capable of seating everyone, responding to everyone, no matter who they are and what burdens they bear. So, too, for our service of *Yizkor*. We sit at this *seder* of *Yizkor* with our Father in Heaven, *avinu sheh-ba-shamayim*, at its head. None of us are the same, nor need be. Though joined by loss, each of us exists somewhere different on this path of grief and recovery. The promise of *Yizkor* is the promise of the *seder;* no matter who we are, there is a place for us waiting, a *makom* with our name on it – *barukh ha-makom* – a blessed God of *neḥama*. *Hamakom yenaḥem etkhem*. The table is set, the moment of *Yizkor* has arrived.

Aḥarei Mot/Kedoshim
"Steamships and Start-ups"

Tomorrow afternoon, t-ball, soccer practice, and other parenting responsibilities permitting, I hope to stop by a one-day conference being hosted at Central Synagogue. I encourage you to attend. If you're interested, speak to Cantor Elana Rozenfeld, who will be going with a group of our congregants. The conference is entitled "Empowered Judaism: How to Build Vibrant Jewish Communities." The sessions are being run by an organization called Mechon Hadar, perhaps the most well-known of a movement of grassroots communities that has flourished across North America. In a time when Jews are full of complaints about the crisis of Jewish continuity, when synagogues are shuttering, UJA's tightening their belts, and movements contracting, these innovative prayer communities, often called independent *minyanim*, have sprung up nationwide, in church basements, co-op party rooms, and even the libraries of long established synagogues. On any given Shabbat, you can walk into the Hadar *minyan* on the West Side, or, for that matter, any number of *minyanim* in Manhattan filled with 20- to 30-somethings – Orthodox, Reform, Conservative or without a label – engaged in vibrant, dynamic, and soulful prayer. They are do-it-yourself communities, a delightful spark of energy for Jewish communal life.

The rub is that as these scrappy *minyanim* are breathing life into our people, many steamships of North American Jewry are gasping for air, searching for answers of how to build vibrant communities. There are those who see the pluck and success of these independent *minyanim* and believe that they somehow detract from the main show, taking away from the institutions that got us this far. Jews, the thinking goes, are cutting off our noses to spite our face, working at odds from within, missing the bigger picture. The intrigue of tomorrow's conference is that it is hosted at one such steamship of New York City Jewish life – Central Synagogue – and, at least on paper, brings these two social forces into the same room. the steamship and the start-up.

The issue is complex and sensitive, and it represents a much bigger question, a question not about prayer, but about community. The same dynamic that I just described regarding prayer could also be described regarding philanthropy. The argument for giving to a centralized agency like UJA or JTS gets harder and harder to make every year, especially as you speak to younger generations. People want to give to their private causes, set up their private foundations. Why give to a faceless place that will then decide how to allocate my dollar when I can be a philanthropic start-up? Or education. If I had a dime for every secular Jew I know who meets with a Chabad rabbi in his office, but would never sign up for an adult education class in a synagogue, I would have a lot of dimes. How many women find the time to meet with a private study group with a *rebbetzin* in their living room, but would never be seen at a class in the 92nd Street Y or the JCC? While I am hitting nerves, let me hit the big one, how many resource-rich families in NYC are choosing to privately tutor their children rather than throw their *yarmulke* in the ring, register their children in a congregational school, and, yes, insist that the program adapts and improves, but not by opting out, but by opting in and making changes from within.

You see, the issue is not an issue of prayer, philanthropy, or education, or at least not entirely. The problem is one of community and meaning. There is an allure to the one-on-one experience, the individualization, the engaged interactive relationship, the boutique experience, the personal trainer feeling, whatever that rabbi-in-my-living-room feeling is that we all love. It makes us feel good, it makes us feel wanted, it makes us feel invested, it makes us feel needed. It makes us feel, well, human. However much we may enjoy the big communal experiences, the baseball and football games, the drama of a full synagogue with a cantor with a beautiful voice chanting *Kol Nidre*, those experiences run the risk of being cavernous and cold. After all, we are anonymous, nobody would know if we are missing, would they? Will they even notice if I don't send my check in? So you know what – we don't and often times they, whoever the they is, don't notice.

If I had to put this discussion into philosophic terms, I would say it is somewhat, but not precisely, a conversation about individualism and communitarianism, a debate between social and political philosophers like John Rawls, Michael Sandel, Michael Walzer, and Amitai Etzion. One side makes a hero of personal choice, of autonomy, of prizing the individual. The other side emphasizes the needs of the community, that while we may value the right to choose our interests and desires, there is a greater good, a greater community of greater value than individual needs. There are centrifugal forces pushing outward towards autonomy and centripetal forces pushing to the center.

One need not look further than today's Torah reading to see these forces play off one another in the most famous ritual of all, the Yom Kippur ceremony led by the high priest Aaron, purgation rites atoning not only for his sins and the sins of his household, but for the sins of all of Israel. It is fascinating to think about. What could be more personal, more private, more sensitive than one's sins, transgressions, and shortcomings? Yet they are expiated in a public and communal fashion. The individual and the communal strike a balance or, more precisely, they are interdependent. Individual values are constructed by way of communal association, in this case the value of acknowledging the common fact of human shortcoming, and the communal need to turn a new page. It may be a powerful experience to confess sin privately, but the Jewish ethic from the Bible to our contemporary Yom Kippur seems to be that we engage in these rituals as a community. There is a reason, the rabbis explain, why our Torah reading devoted to personal ethics, *Kedoshim*, begins in the plural – *Kedoshim t'hiyu*, "You (plural) shall be holy." While values can only be held by individuals, they are shaped, inculcated, reinforced, and passed on by communities. We need both, the individual and the community, the centripetal and centrifugal, the start-up and the steamship. Too much of one leads to inertia and anonymity, whereas too much of the other leads to fragmentation and isolation. It is a balancing act.

I can think of no more compelling conversation than this to lead here at Park Avenue Synagogue. If there was ever a congregation that is perceived as a "steamship" of North American Jewry, we are it. We have cantors with big voices, schools with big enrollments, rabbis who like to give long sermons, a Sisterhood, a Men's Club, all the bells and whistles of large congregational life. Even our name, "Park Avenue Synagogue," evinces a certain something. That claim is more than superficial. We have a responsibility to be a flagship for Jewish music, Jewish thought, Jewish philanthropy, and Torah. But what would be even more interesting to me would be for this synagogue to lead a cultural conversation, or more importantly, to exemplify a congregational model that encourages a conversation about the interplay between the individual and the community, a congregation that practices innovation and that brings a scrappy, gumption-filled "let's try something new" attitude to these hallowed halls.

I can imagine a world where a rabbi teaches a class to lay educators, who are then empowered to lead *ḥavurot* in people's homes. A place where Hebrew school teachers teach children in the classroom one day and on another day meet with a group of parents in their homes, because what we really want are parents who are able to talk to their children about Jewish content. Where some Shabbat dinner programs involve bringing in big speakers, and others involve a different sort of scholar-in-residence. That scholar is you – a mother or father in his or her own home – given the tools to celebrate Shabbat by the synagogue. I can imagine a community with a congregational choir that doesn't perform only on holidays, but is strategically placed in this sanctuary, working closely with the cantor, infusing this space with confident song as a new melody is introduced on any given Shabbat. I can imagine a sort of synergy whereby a *ḥavurah* service is viewed not so much as an alternative to the main service, but rather as a welcome opportunity to impact the synagogue as a whole.

Some things in this world are given. There will be a rabbi and a cantor here, the architecture of the sanctuary will not change, and there will be a *Kol Nidre* appeal. There are limits, of budget and of staff. We cannot, nor should we, strive to be all things to all people. There must be a center, a coherent vision, a brand, a *torah* of Park

Avenue Synagogue, as I like to say. At the same time, our imaginations must be supple and elastic. If this community were able to find a way to harness and leverage the creative tension of autonomy and community, of start-up and steamship, not only would we be far more than the sum of our parts, but we would actually be providing a working solution to one of the big, elephant-in-the-room questions facing American Jewry.

The debate between individualism and community is ongoing and recurrent. As with the debate over cuffs on men's slacks or skirt length for women, I can promise you that what is fashionable today may be out tomorrow. For every mega-church there is an independent *minyan*, for every turn inward, there is a reflex to be part of something bigger. It is not a debate that will ever be won, which is, of course, the very point. The successful communities, and I hope ours will be counted as such, will be the ones that recognize this fact early on, and rather than debating the relative merits of one side or the other, commit to using the energy of both towards enhancing our community, enhancing ourselves as individuals, and enhancing the relationships with each other and with our common God that make us each Holy.

Emor

"Pesaḥ Sheni: Second Chances"

It may come to you as a surprise to hear that this past week you missed a Jewish holiday. Not just any festival, not some newfangled new age observance begun in the past few years or even centuries, but as Judaism goes, as ancient as ancient gets – all the way back to the time of Moses and the Torah. Last Wednesday, April 28th, corresponding to the 14th day of the Hebrew month of Iyar, the Jewish people (or at least one or two of them) observed something called *Pesaḥ sheni*, the second Passover. If you missed it, don't beat yourself up too much, it's as minor a festival as they come, but I think you will find that its message extends well beyond its limited and modest beginnings.

About one month ago, we gathered around our *seder* tables to celebrate Passover. The biblical text is very clear: on the 14th day of the Hebrew month of Nisan, the Passover Sacrifice was to be performed, an act that we continue to commemorate on this date every year. Among the wandering Israelites, however, there were those who, for unavoidable reasons, were in a state of ritual impurity on that day and were thus unable to offer the Passover sacrifice. They became distraught at having missed this sacred observance. In response, Moses legislated a law stating that should any Israelite be unable to celebrate Passover, due to ritual impurity, because of having been detained on a long journey, or because of volcanic ash (well, it didn't say that), then they were to be given a second opportunity, a second Passover, exactly one month later. On that day, the 14th day of Iyar, which fell last Wednesday, they could celebrate a "make-up festival." (Numbers 9:1-14)

It is an extraordinary concept – a holiday that seems to be all about mulligans and "do overs." These days, there is really nothing to do on *Pesaḥ sheni* other than finish off any *matzah* remaining in our cupboards, but the very concept is enough to give us pause, to think about second chances, a unique message in the history of religions.

It is difficult, without a doubt, to give someone a second chance – maybe that's why we need a holiday about it. If you've been let down by someone, have been wronged, directly or indirectly, with malice or by accident, to give that person another chance, you have to dig deep. This is not a sermon about forgiveness; that is a sermon for another day. We Jews talk about repentance and forgiveness an awful lot, especially around the High Holy Days. Today I want to talk to you about a different muscle group, related but slightly more subtle and perhaps harder to access: the ability to, when wronged, simply move on, get over it, and press forward with a relationship.

To see past someone's flaws, what the Talmud calls *ma'avir al middotav*, is hardly a natural instinct. If a person meant to wrong us, then goodbye and good riddance, at least until that person decides to eat crow and beg for forgiveness. If they didn't mean it, well they should have known better. I have had occasion to share my favorite story about Simon Wiesenthal, the famous Nazi-hunter who passed away a few years ago. He tells of the days following the war, when a neighbor approached him and asked "Could you lend me ten dollars until Monday? I've got a package coming tomorrow. I'll sell it on the black market; Monday, you'll have your money back. I swear it." Wiesenthal figured, "Why not help out a neighbor? I'll lend him the money." Monday arrived, the man came up to him and said, "I don't know what happened. The package didn't arrive. You know how messed up the mail is these days. But don't worry; it'll be here any day." This went on for weeks. Twice a week, for six weeks, the man came up with one excuse or another. Finally after six weeks, the man came to Wiesenthal and said, "It came. I sold it. Here's the ten dollars you lent me." And Wiesenthal answered, "No, keep it. For ten dollars, it's not worth changing my opinion of you."

It's a great story, but it makes us laugh because we know deep down that Wiesenthal was wrong. Wiesenthal owed his neighbor, he owed himself, the opportunity to rise above the particulars of that disappointment. Not for ten dollars, not for any price, is it worth allowing a single moment of disenchantment to overshadow the breadth of an entire relationship. We owe others, we owe ourselves second chances.

There are times, of course, when people should not be given a second chance. Not everything should be forgiven and not every moment is a teachable moment. There are wrongs that can't be made right, offenses that cannot be mitigated. No two people are the same, every relationship is unique. What one relationship can overcome can be debilitating to another. I am sure there are times when the magnitude of the wrong or its persistent nature is of such a degree that it is not in anyone's interest to move forward. Whether it's between colleagues, spouses, family members or countries, there are times when a misdeed can eclipse the totality of a relationship.

But here's the thing. As I see it, there are two givens in this world. First and foremost, human imperfection. None of us is without fault. As sure as I am that everyone in this room has been wronged by someone, I am doubly sure that everyone in this room, myself included, knows of a time when he or she has, knowingly or unknowingly, hurt someone. The second given is that human beings must exist in relationship with other human beings. These relationships – casual or profound, biological, collegial, or otherwise – are the foundations of our identity. As human beings we need sustained contact with others.

The math is actually straightforward. If we are all imperfect and we all exist in relation to others, then it is simply impossible to go very far in this world without encountering another person's faults and shortcomings. In fact, I would go so far as to say that it is altogether unhealthy to think that any human being – our parents, our mentors, and certainly we ourselves – is perfect. Because if you do, when that person does let you down, which they will because they are, after all, human, your excessive estimation will crash like a house of cards.

This is why second chances are so important. Somewhere between a do nothing, "let bygones be bygones" and a full act of forgiveness and reconciliation exists a very important and courageous middle ground: the ability to see and acknowledge hurt, absorb it and move past it. It is not about amnesia, not about excusing, condoning, mitigating, or contextualizing, rather, it is a form of amnesty. Think of post-Apartheid South Africa. I believe there is healing that comes by way of making the conscious decision not to live a life of regret or resentment. To let the future reign over the past. We examine the past, accept it for what it was, and move forward in earnest caution towards a greater good.

Just this past week a congregant came to me in anger. She had been let down by the synagogue, felt mistreated, a feeling made all the worse by this person's deep love of the community. I listened to her describe how a bad situation was mishandled, how words were not carefully chosen, how messages were muddled. It was interesting, because once she had said her piece and spoken her mind, it was clear this person was not looking for an apology. The deed was done, it would never, by definition, happen again. When I had heard her out and validated that feeling, we arrived at an awkward pause. I didn't know what to say, so I asked, "So where do we go from here?" To which she replied, "Now we move forward." In the grand scheme of things the incident was minor, but the lesson this person taught me – to vent, take a breath and extend a second chance, in this case, to the synagogue – is one that we all need to learn and a capacity that we all need to cultivate. As Rabbi Joseph Soloveitchik wrote, "Sin… can be transformed…. into the guiding hand of the future, into a source of merit and good deeds." (*Halakhic Man*, pp. 116-117).

Once upon a time there was a king who ruled a small kingdom. It wasn't all that great a kingdom, nor was it well-known for any of its resources or its people. But the king owned a diamond, a great and perfect diamond that had been in his family for generations. He kept it on display for all to see and appreciate. People came from all over the world to admire it and gaze upon it. One day a guard came to the king with the news that, although no one had touched the precious stone, for it was always guarded, the diamond was cracked. The king ran to see, and sure enough, there was a crack right through the middle of the diamond. Immediately the king summoned all the jewelers of the land and had them look at the jewel. One after another they examined it and gave the king the same bad news: the diamond was irrevocably flawed. The king was crushed and so were his subjects. They felt that they had lost everything.

Then, out of nowhere, came an old man who claimed be a jeweler. He asked to see the diamond. After examining it, he looked up and confidently told the king. "I can fix it. In fact, I can make it better than before." Although the king was a bit leery, he allowed the old man to work on the jewel. He placed the old man in a room with tools and gave him food and drink for a week. At the end of the week the man appeared with the stone in his hand and gave it to the king. The king couldn't believe his eyes. It was magnificent! The old man had fixed it, and he had made it even better than it had been before! He had used the crack that ran through the middle of the stone as a stem and had carved an intricate full-blown rose, leaves and thorns into the diamond. It was exquisite. The king was overjoyed and offered the man half of his kingdom. The old man refused and said "All I did was to take something flawed and cracked at its heart and turn it into something beautiful."

There is no life, there is no relationship that is without flaw. We all have shortcomings, disappointment, pain, and loss. Sometimes you can make a rose from the flaw, sometimes you just have to let go of the diamond, and sometimes, just sometimes, you discover that it is that very flaw that makes you who you are and to efface it is to lose the very thing that makes you, 'you.' Only the person who acknowledges the imperfections and scars and cracks within is able to become complete. It is not enough simply to identify faults. As we have fallen short in the past, we can now aspire to greater heights, to be better people, to reinvent ourselves and our relationships in ways we never imagined possible; in other words, to give second chances. Life is simply too short to do otherwise.

B'har/B'ḥukkotai
"A Narrow Bridge"

Kol ha-olam kulo gesher tzar m'od v'ha-ikkar lo l'faḥed klal. "The whole world is a very narrow bridge, and the essential thing is not to fear at all."

These words, adapted from the writings of the great Hassidic master Rabbi Naḥman of Bratzlav, are as enigmatic as they are famous. Set to music, the words are sung by children in schools and summer camps, at *b'nei mitzvah* celebrations, weddings, *Shabbat* tables, in every Jewish setting imaginable – by me, by you, probably many times over. What is interesting is that I have never stopped to consider what message the lyrics are actually communicating. "The whole world is a very narrow bridge, and the essential thing is not to fear at all." Why is the world like a bridge, a narrow one at that, and if it is, why not fear – especially if you are doing something dangerous, like crossing a narrow bridge?

After a week like this one, a month like this one, I found myself lingering on the haunting melody, humming it to myself, thinking about the words and their meaning. As New Yorkers, we continue to feel a collective sigh of relief after dodging a potential terrorist bomb in Times Square last Saturday night. Just imagine what could have happened, the death and destruction, the unraveling of our safety net. We are deeply alert to the sense of good fortune, luck,

---

I would like to thank Rabbi Harold Kushner for his explicit and implicit influence on this sermon. After a lifetime of admiration from afar, I was finally able to make his acquaintance this past year and I dedicate the above sermon to his ongoing influence. Anyone interested in an extended meditation on living in an uncertain world would do well to read Rabbi Kushner's recently released book, Conquering Fear: Living Boldly in an Uncertain World *(Knopf, 2009).*

or blessing that we avoided an attack by the skin of our teeth. We are grateful for the collective forces that, just in the nick of time, were able to stop this would-be terrorist from completing his mission. We all feel thankful that we have walked this bridge to safety. Nevertheless, even having arrived, we are equally aware, as demonstrated by yesterday's evacuation, of just how narrow that bridge is, how close we are to the edge, and how easy it would been to fall off.

The simple truth is that for every Times Square "exhale," every near miss, we have far too many reminders of late that more often than not we actually do slip off. The oil rig explosion that has wreaked havoc on the Gulf of Mexico, a horrific and long-term ecological disaster – such a tragic loss, just weeks after one of the worst coal mining disasters in history. Every few days I hear of another earthquake. If there ever was a time that we felt battered and buffeted, not totally in control of the events of our lives, this is it. What about that volcano? Have we forgotten already? If you want to hear from someone who felt their destiny was not their own, controlled by forces beyond our power – speak to someone who was stuck in Europe that week.

The shocks are not only geological. There are also political and economic shake-ups – the elections in the United Kingdom and the riots in Greece. I was speaking to a friend in the financial world and he reflected that this week, people went to sleep simply not knowing what the next day would bring, not knowing how far the Greek meltdown would spread, and how long it would last – a very narrow Wall Street, perhaps even a tightrope, that many, perhaps many in this room, continue to walk. We want to be in control, we work hard to direct the events of our lives, but a week like this is a not-so-gentle reminder that however hard we try, no matter how tightly we seek to grip our reality, it is simply not for us to predict, and certainly not for us to determine, the script of this uncertain world. As the Yiddish proverb goes: *A mensch tracht un Gott lacht,* Man plans and God laughs.

The awareness that we live in an unpredictable and uncontrollable world, a world shot through with contingency, is hardly new to us. If anything, the question of how to progress through a world that is ultimately not ours to understand or control is one that our predecessors asked with far greater frequency than we do. Arguably, the ancients approached this question with greater sincerity and deeper humility, if for no other reason than that they were not filled with our modern presumption that one *can* control his or her surroundings. We in this room delude ourselves thinking that we are in control, unaware of the fact that we are one volcano, one computer crash away from being stopped in our tracks. To use a trivial example: just yesterday, the synagogue's tech person informed us that our computers would need to be shut down for an hour. It was totally disorienting. I found myself doing something very late 90's – using a telephone. We produce medical advances and technological innovation; we try to tighten our grip ever so slightly, but it is only a tweak at the edges. The fundamental limitations and frailties of what it is to be human remain constant.

Think about our *parasha*, a bold statement reminding us that it is not we who hold the cards. There is the *shmittah*, the sabbatical year that took place every seven years, when slaves went free and the land lay fallow. There is the jubilee year that took place after seven sabbatical cycles, when everyone went free and all non-urban land reverted back to its ancestral family's possession. Rabbi Abraham Isaac Kook explained that the jubilee year is a spiritual regimen to engender a sense of humility before an unknowable God. We let the land lie fallow because doing so cultivates and strengthens this sense of humility. We do not have the final say.

Blessings and curses abound, and we, living from one moment to the next, do not know what is in store. This brings us to the central question at hand. If we are not in control, and if we don't know what will happen from one moment to the next, how do we proceed? If the world is such a narrow bridge, how do we walk it, if we walk it at all?

The answer, or at least part of the answer, is in the song: *lo l'faḥed klal*. We do not fear, or at least we do not allow our fear to immobilize us. In other words we "walk on." As Rabbi Harold Kushner explains: "Courage is not the absence of fear; it is the overcoming of fear." (*Conquering Fear*, p. 168) Even in the face of the unknown, we press forward with cautious optimism, alert but not frightened, vigilant but not paranoid.

Illness, Mother Nature, and a deeply flawed humanity – these are narrow bridges of uncertainty in all of our futures. It never has been and never will be for us to control our surroundings. What is in our power is to choose to leverage that uncertainty towards cultivating a profound appreciation for the present blessings of our lives. We need to hug our children in a way that treasures the moment, but never so tightly that they fail to develop their own self-confidence in this uncertain world that will be theirs to inherit. None of us need look far to be reminded of our mortality. But the choice of what we do with that awareness belongs to us, we dare not be paralyzed for fear of falling – we can and must make the willed choice to cross these bridges before us. As Eleanor Roosevelt wrote, "You gain strength, courage and confidence by every experience in which you stop to look fear in the face and you are able to say to yourself, 'I lived through this... I can take the next thing that comes along.' You must do the thing you think you cannot do." (quoted in Kushner, *Conquering Fear*, pp. 170-171)

It was none other than our own late Rabbi Milton Steinberg who recognized that greater than the fear of death is the fear of life. That far too many of us go through this world with a temerity born of a fear of the unknown, the "what ifs" and the inevitable uncertainties of our existence. Faced with this fear, Steinberg taught, we must choose to proceed with a sense of purposeful duty. In Steinberg's words: "Let the mother tend her young and let the poet sing his song, and the laborer dig his ditch and the merchant do his best. And if life is hard and the child grows into an ungrateful [adult] and the poet's song falls on deaf ears, if the laborer digs his ditch in vain and the merchant fails in his business endeavors, then at least each will have done his or her duty." (quoted in Kushner, *Conquering Fear*, p. 171)

Our lives are indeed akin to standing on a narrow bridge. If we stand still, we shall be frozen. If we veer too far to the left or to the right we shall most certainly fall and be dashed to pieces. What we must do, wrote William James, is to "'Be strong and of a good courage.' Act for the best, hope for the best, and take what comes... If death ends all, we cannot meet death better." (Conclusion of his essay "The Will to Believe")

Kol ha-olam kulo gesher tzar m'od v'ha-ikkar lo l'faḥed klal. "The whole world is a very narrow bridge, and the essential thing is not to fear at all." I think, finally, I know what it means. May we – this week, next week and the years ahead – live up to Reb Naḥman's charge, believing in ourselves, believing in our God, believing that our lives, precarious as they are, can be lived hopefully, courageously, and filled with purpose.

B'midbar

"Kugel on a Hot Sommer Day"

If every single Jewish studies professor, from every campus across North America, were to get on an airplane that took off, flew away, and never came back again, would Jewish life change at all? Our synagogues, our Hebrew Schools, our Jewish summer camps, our UJA's, our relationship with Israel – if there were no Jewish studies departments on campus, would it have any effect on the Jewish community? I remember being asked this question by a Jewish communal professional some time ago while I was working on my doctorate in Jewish studies. He conjured up this scenario to illustrate that the impact of such a development on Jewish life would be negligible. He felt that Jewish studies professors, Jewish studies departments, the scientific study of Judaism – in German, *Wissenschaft des Judentums* – has absolutely no positive impact on religious life whatsoever.

I ruminated on this question this past week as I led a discussion of Jewish studies professors under the auspices of the Hartman Institute in Jerusalem. This year I was appointed to the North American Scholars Circle, involving bimonthly conference calls among Jewish academics from across North America, an honor made that much more humbling as I am the only pulpit rabbi in the group. The academic discussions, which will culminate in a week-long seminar in Jerusalem this summer, serve as an opportunity for Jewish studies professors to learn together, to reflect on and sharpen their craft, build dialogue, and address some of the most pressing Jewish questions of our day.

Last week, it was my turn to present. I chose to teach a debate taking place in the academic world specifically on the pages of the

Jewish Quarterly Review (JQR), a debate that I think goes to the heart of my colleague's airplane question. Don't beat yourself up if you haven't heard about it – JQR's readership is slightly less than *Time* or *Newsweek*.

James Kugel, one of the most well-respected professors of Hebrew Bible, wrote a book a few years ago called *How to Read the Bible*. What makes Kugel and the book interesting is that Kugel is an Orthodox Jew, yet he has spent his entire career studying the Torah as a critical scholar. As a Jew he treats the Torah as a sacred text, to be read reverentially and approached devotionally, reflecting the will of God. In fact, much of his career has been devoted to studying how the Bible has been read over the ages by religious communities, Jewish and otherwise. Yet, as an academic, Kugel publishes and teaches that the Bible is of human origin, a product of the Ancient Near East, full of contradictions, flawed and imperfect. So there are two Kugels, the Kugel who treats the Bible as an artifact of the ancient world and the Kugel who treats the Bible as a divinely given text. For Kugel, the controversy of his book is that he believes that these two worlds, the world of scholarship and Bible as artifact and the world of devotional study and Bible as sacred scripture, can never be reconciled. The claims of one impugn on the other. In fact, to mix the two undercuts the integrity of each project. True scholarship cannot be bound by religious commitments as it must be objective, unbiased, and without an end in mind. Religious life operates on opposite principles; it cannot accept any findings of critical scholarship that may dethrone the place of Torah in the Jewish mind.

In comes Benjamin Sommer, a JTS professor, a fine scholar and a religious Jew, who published an article this past spring in JQR taking Kugel to task for his approach. Sommer accuses Kugel of having a bifurcated soul. Sommer argues that scholarship can and should inform religious life, that proving the human hand in the Biblical text does not undercut religious life, rather, it enhances it. Kugel, Sommer claims, does his readers a disservice by insisting that one cannot treat the Bible as an artifact and as sacred scripture at the same time. To use but one example from Sommer's work, some time ago he wrote an article about the book of Numbers, the book of the Bible that we began today. He demonstrates that within this book, there are series of inconsistencies and internal contradictions, about Moses' character, about the nature of God's holiness, about many things; contradictions that prove that the text was written by many hands. Yet these contradictions are not whimsical, they are purposeful, they are retained by a careful editor, intent on maintaining certain tensions within a unified text. For Sommer, the scholarship informs the sacred character of the text. In fact, Sommer explains in an unusually personal footnote for a scholarly article, it was exactly when he learned that maybe the Torah is not from God, that he stopped eating cheeseburgers. In a somewhat unexpected logic, to learn the Torah is only human can actually bring you closer to the divine voice behind it.

In such a short time, it is impossible to delve into all the particulars of the debate, and I am giving them short shrift as it is. The essential element is the airplane question with which I started. Does scholarship inform Jewish life? Sommer says yes, it actually enhances, deepens, and elevates our relationship to Torah and Judaism. Kugel says no, scholarship and Judaism must exist as separate spheres. For Sommer, all those Jewish studies professors can, at least theoretically, contribute mightily to the Jewish community. For Kugel, that airplane of Jewish professors, while costing him his day job, would not impact the devotional study of Torah.

The debate is not an abstract ivory tower discussion. The debate goes directly to the guts of who we are as a community, what we believe in, and how those beliefs should be communicated. Just this week, one of the teachers in our schools stopped me in the hallway. The children are of course preparing for the festival of Shavuot, the holiday that commemorates God's giving of the Torah to Israel at Mount Sinai. The teacher confided in me that she knew what the traditional explanation of the festival was, but she also knew her history, and she didn't feel comfortable teaching her kids a story that contradicted everything she knew from biology, geology, anthropology, psychology, to name just a few contemporary disciplines. How should I answer her? Does a parochial religious education require that you, as Kugel would advise, put your intellectual commitments on hold? If we teach a secular truth, will our children grow up with no reverence for their heritage?

It is a difficult question, one that has a long history with implications that range from how to teach the Torah and campus life to Jewish philanthropy. Jewish studies is a relatively new discipline – only about 200 years old. When the academic study of Judaism began in 19th-century Germany, it was part of the project of Emancipation, an attempt to make Jewish study kosher, as it were, in the eyes of the non-Jewish world. Judaism could be studied objectively, and professors of Jewish studies could be full and dignified participants in Western intellectual life. Two hundred years later, the landscape is vastly different. There are Jewish studies departments everywhere. Jewish philanthropists give huge amounts of money to endow chairs of Jewish study to keep the study of Judaism vibrant and to give our undergrads a place to study their heritage on campus. In my years at the University of Chicago, Jewish kids would ask me all the time how it was that I, a religious Jew, could teach the "Who Wrote the Bible?" class. And remember, what gives Jewish studies professors tenure is not how many Jewish souls they've saved, but how many papers they've published and how many conferences they've attended. I wouldn't be the Jew I am if it weren't for the Jewish studies departments at the University of Michigan, at the University of Chicago, and beyond. But consider the irony: Jewish philanthropists support academics in order to passionately revive Jewish life – the same academics who live or die by being dispassionate with their material and their students.

I don't have all the answers, not even close. Kugel and Sommer are a lot smarter than we'll ever be. If they are out there debating, then I am not sure we are going to resolve this question. That said, we are responsible for this institution; we are responsible for the Torah that is taught here. On the one hand, I understand Kugel's position. The moment a scholar ceases being totally objective, he ceases being a scholar. Moreover, the moment a Jew allows for the presence of a human hand in sacred texts, the genie is out of the bottle, and the white knuckle grip the Torah has on you is, inevitably, a little looser. That said, there is simply no way I could ever preach, teach, or construct a model of Jewish education that did not allow for the asking of any and every question, for grappling with the answers to those questions, and for the answers to inform our vision of Jewish life. As Sommer, Krochmal, and others have argued, if I discover that "By the rivers of Babylon" was not really written by King David or that Isaiah did not write "Comfort ye, comfort ye My people," then so be it. A lobotomized faith is not an option for me. I choose a mature, textured faith; a messy, unresolved faith with all its internal contradictions; a faith that seeks to come to grips with the competing tugs at my identity, my heart and my mind, the academy, and the pulpit, the human and divine elements of our tradition. When it comes to faith, the mark of integrity has nothing to do with being neat and tidy. The mark of integrity is standing before your God knowing you have brought every question you have to the table.

In the days before Shavuot, as important as it is to ask these questions, we can also be satisfied without having definite answers. However, we do need answers or at least the right way to model them. In the end, the answer that I gave the teacher, and really all our schools was an unexpected one, one that had been fortuitously planned by Rabbi Rein and our schools.

This past year, we discovered that owing to wear and tear, some of our Torah scrolls needed repairs. Rabbi Rein hired a *sofer*, a trained scribe, to fix our Torah scrolls. But instead of doing what a scribe normally does – taking the scrolls to his own workshop, or setting up shop in a hidden classroom – our *sofer*, Jay Greenspan, asked to sit in a high traffic area. He set up his workspace outside the elevator on the second floor. Over the last week, every class, every student – from the ECC through the Congregational School – had the opportunity to watch him and to learn from him about his work.

That is my answer to the teacher and her students. That is my answer, because I imagine that in seeing the scribe at work, our children took in, without words, and in an age-appropriate way, the exact message they needed to hear. They saw the Torah up close, a covenantal document given by God, written by humans, handed down through the ages, kept up and cared for by every generation. This is what was taught this week in our schools, this is my answer to the teachers, to Kugel and to Sommer. The rest, as they say, is commentary.

Shavuot, Second Day
"*Yizkor: Retrieving the Past*"

I want to tell you a story about something wonderful that happened to me this past week, very possibly the nicest thing that has happened to me in a long time. It's a true story, a story-inside-a-story that will require a bit of patience on your part, but I promise it will be well worth it. It will hopefully inspire you on this festival of Shavuot and provide you the tools to prepare for the *Yizkor* service which will begin in just a few minutes.

The story begins with an unexpected question – one that is appropriate for this time of year: What is the most exciting moment in baseball history of the last 25 years, if not ever? Not Larsen's perfect game, not Bobby Thompson's three-run homer over the Giants, not Mazeroski's leadoff home run. I'll give you a hint – I grew up in Los Angeles. The answer of course is Kirk Gibson's ninth inning home run off Dennis Eckersley of the Oakland A's in game 1 of the '88 World Series. The Dodgers were one run down. With Mike Davis on base, 2 outs, Gibson came up to bat, with both legs injured and nursing a stomach virus. Davis stole second, the count was full. The pitch was a backdoor slider, and Gibson hit it straight into the right field bleachers – a home run to win the game, a scene made famous as Gibson pumped his fists against the backdrop of all the tail lights of the disheartened LA fans who had already left the stadium trying to beat traffic. I was there that night, cheering in the bleachers. It was, without a doubt, the most exciting sporting moment I have ever watched, made even sweeter because I shared it with my dad, who is here today. Ever since then, among all my sports heroes, Kirk Gibson has always held a special place in my heart.

Some years later, I became a rabbi and as anyone who has sat in my office knows, my office is full of baseballs, some signed and some just for fun. Aside from reflecting my love of baseball, they are there so that fidgety *b'nei mitzvah* kids have something to hold onto, a conversation piece as they sit nervously in the Rabbi's office.

Years ago, while I was in Chicago, one such student, her name was Jenna, came to my office. She sat there looking at the baseballs and began to tell me about her *mitzvah* project for her upcoming *bat mitzvah*. She too loved baseball, and had a hobby of collecting players' signatures. For her *bat mitzvah* she initiated a letter campaign to major league players to sign baseballs – baseballs she auctioned on eBay to raise money for special needs children's programs. She ended up raising about $8000. I recall being awed by her determination, and I told her that there was only one signed baseball I really wanted – Kirk Gibson. I regaled her with the story in much greater detail than I gave you this morning, impressing upon her the mythic place Gibson has in my heart. Now, Jenna knew her business and explained that Gibson doesn't sign baseballs. His signature is one of the hardest to get. The two of us left the matter there.

Jenna grew up, I moved to New York and the story, I thought, was over. Until last week. Last week a box arrived at the synagogue. I had no idea what it was. I opened it and pulled out a baseball – not just any baseball, but a signed baseball: "To Rabbi. My best. Kirk Gibson." The note that came with it was the best part, of course. From Jenna, now grown up, explaining that she didn't forget. A few weeks ago she was at a Cubs game against the Diamondbacks. She saw Gibson, now a bench coach for Arizona. She held up a sign asking him for a signature. He saw it. Jenna explained to him what a Rabbi is and instructed him how to spell it: R-A-B-B-I. He signed it, she sent it to me... and here it is. It feels every bit as good as I thought it would.

In fact, it is even better. What a feeling! I imagined that I would always be able to recall this resourceful student, but with the passing of time and the shift in geography, the immediacy of the relationship would understandably be moderated. So what she did – retrieving our exchange, having stored it, as it were, in the active file, and responding years later with a singular gesture of kindness and generosity – is an act that I will forever treasure. The Gibson baseball is nice, as is the humbling reward that I had an impact on the life of an impressionable Jewish teen. But the ripple effect of the entire incident extends much wider, and reaches deeper. With the arrival of the gift, past and present collapsed into one sublime moment; memories from twenty-five years ago and from a handful of years ago, all brought into sharp relief.

On this festival of Shavuot, it is precisely this feeling that we are all called on to access, in response to the arrival of a very different gift, the Torah, a sacred gift from the Divine Giver. The students of the Kotzker Rebber asked him why Shavuot is called "the time the Torah was given," rather than "the time we received the Torah"? The Rebbe answered that "indeed the giving of the Torah took place on one day, but the receiving of the Torah takes place across time, in fact, at all times." The festival of Shavuot, or for that matter, almost every Jewish holiday operates on a very particular metaphysical calculus. The event we are commemorating – in today's case, revelation, the giving of the Torah – is located in our temporal past. Like the ball game, like the sharp *bat mitzvah* student, it happened and we are profoundly grateful for the experience. But the promise of Shavuot is not so much about revelation past, as about revelation renewed, not about history but about retrieval. When we take the Torah out of the Ark, every time, especially at Shavuot, we are asked to hear the sound of Sinai with immediacy and even with intimacy as if, in the language of Franz Rosenzweig, the voice of God is speaking directly to us.

Rosenzweig's elder contemporary Martin Buber perhaps best understood that who we are as Jews hinges on our ability to retrieve our sacred past into the fabric of our contemporary present. For Martin Buber, the renewal of Judaism could never happen through nationalism, erudition, or by adoption of a set of creeds or ritual practices. Embedded within each of us, both individually and as a community, exists a deeper Jewish consciousness, a *pintele yid*, that waits to be renewed. A vital Jewish identity comes by way of the spiritual process whereby this spark is retrieved, stoked, and affirmed. For Buber, Jewish renewal has nothing to do with reconfiguring or reformulating Judaism to suit faddish needs of the present. Renewal happens by connecting the alienated Jew to the promises and events of the

Jewish past and making that past one's present. The significance of Shavuot is that it insists on reintegrating the receiving of Torah into the life of every contemporary Jew.

This reintegration, I believe, is the reason why we read the book of Ruth on Shavuot. Every other Jewish journey of note involves a journey forward to somewhere new, into the unknown. The expulsion of Adam and Eve from the Garden of Eden, Abraham and Sarah's call to go forth to Canaan, Joseph's descent to Egypt, Jonah's ill-advised flight to Tarshish, and of course the Israelites' journey to the Promised Land. Only in the book of Ruth is the journey a story of return: Naomi going back to the land of Judah. The story of Naomi and Ruth is appropriate for Shavuot precisely because it is a story of return, geographically, but more importantly, a reconnection with the past; about how a person, alienated and estranged can be brought back into the fold, restored, and reconstituted amongst her people. This is why the Torah is called the inheritance of the house of Jacob, *morasha Kehillat Ya'akov*. Shavuot is not about new knowledge, it is about reclaiming something that is our birthright, a gift of Torah that has always existed in the substrata of our identity. On this holiday, we are asked to bring out what has always been ours into full view.

It is precisely this act – of receiving a past that lies within and allowing it to inform our present – that *Yizkor* is all about. Yizkor is certainly about the past, about loss, about acknowledging that death has forever distanced us our loved ones from us. Today we remember mothers and fathers, brothers and sisters, husbands, wives, sons and daughters, all our loved ones whose deaths have forever left us unwhole. Each one of us stands incomplete, knowing that those near and dear to us are forever removed from our present. That awareness is disorienting and painful. Last week I spoke to a woman in our community who lost her father some time ago. She shared with me how difficult it is for her that the world moves forward, people move on, but she cannot, because even with the passing of time, even as the immediacy of grief subsides, the loss of a loved one remains. Death is not something that can ever be overcome. The impenetrable and terrible boundary of human mortality is a divide that we can never traverse. This is why we need this moment – this service of *Yizkor*.

Yizkor is our opportunity to retrieve what is ours. The memories of our past are both beyond our reach, yet ours to claim as our rightful and ongoing inheritance. The kindness and wisdom of a parent who continues to shape our moral code; the love of a life partner, who even in his or her absence, informs our very being. The wisdom of a brother or a sister who, even in death, remains our teacher. A child whose life remains for us a testament of love. *Yizkor* is not meant to ease grief. It does not diminish our loss. The power of *Yizkor* is that it teaches us that the lives of our loved ones, while lodged in our past, can and must be a legacy that informs our present and future. The memories of our loved ones can become a blessing when and only when we crack open our hearts and souls just wide enough to allow for the possibility that we can still feel the immediacy of their love, that we can still learn from them, that we the living, while separated from the past, can still draw on it as an ever-renewing source of strength.

William Faulkner wrote, "The past is never dead. It's not even the past." At this time of *Yizkor*, if I were to recast Faulkner in Jewish coin, it would be "The dead even in their passing, are never past." Who we are, what we can be, the degree to which we will live our lives in a manner worthy of remembrance, pivots on our ability to call on the memories of our loved ones, drawing sustenance from them, ever aware of our loss. It is, without a doubt, unexpected to hear that forward momentum, spiritual, personal or otherwise, is propelled by a retrieval of the past. Yet, this is the message of Shavuot, this is what it means to be Jewish, what it means to be human. The time for *Yizkor* has arrived. The time to draw on the past is present.

Beha'alotkha

"What's So Funny About Boycott, Divestment, and Sanctions?"

V*ay'hi binsoa ha-aron, va-yomer Moshe,* When the Ark was carried forward, Moses would declare: "*Kuma Adonai, v'yafutzu oyvekha, v'yanusu m'sanekha mi-panekha,* Arise Lord, may your enemies be scattered, may your foes be put to flight." These words, found in our parasha, *Beha'alotkha,* are sung at the beginning of every single Torah service. They are possibly the most recognizable part of our *tefillah,* connecting our own Torah procession, as it were, to the journeys of the ancient Israelites through the wilderness.

The question is, what do the words mean? "Rise up, let your enemies (*oyvekha*) be scattered, your foes (*m'sanekha*) be put to flight." Why the repetition? Why both "enemies" (*oyvekha*) and "foes" (*m'sanekha*)? Why the two different words, what does one add to the other? Wouldn't one be enough? After all, who needs two different kinds of enemies?

Rashi, the 11th-century commentator, notes the redundancy and unpacks it by way of a *midrash* in the Sifrei (Piska 84). On one level *oyvekha* and *m'sanekha,* "your enemies" and "your foes," are synonymous. Rashi explains that they reflect two very different threats, different, but interconnected and interdependent. The first word, *oyvekha,* is the obvious enemy, what Rashi calls *ham'khunasim.* These are the ones who are literally assembled at your doorstep – an existential threat, a direct menace to your very being. When we think of an enemy, ancient or modern, personal or national, one that presents an immediate danger, this is what usually comes to mind. The second word, *m'sanekha,* is more subtle. Rashi explains that this is "*harodfim.*" These are the ones who are, as it were, snapping at your heels. They are a threat, but not in the same way, not with the same immediacy, as the first group. They assert themselves craftily and with stealth against the Israelites. The Psalmist (Ps. 83) explains that they have made an alliance, "unanimous in their counsel," plotting that "Israel's name be mentioned no more." Their attacks are not so much aimed at Israel's physical being, and their actions are not always explicit – *Al am'kha yarimu sod*, "Against your people they plot secrets." Two different words representing two different groups, both in formation against Israel, connected in their hatred, who, by different methods, work in common cause against our people.

The month of June concludes my second year here at Park Avenue Synagogue. To the extent that anyone is keeping track, you know that when it comes to Israel, while I have spoken on the subject many times, and am very proud of our Israel *Shabbaton*, our planned congregational trips to Israel, our participation last week in the Salute to Israel parade, our communal and cultural celebrations; for the most part, when it comes to Israeli politics, I have held my tongue. I don't speak on Israeli politics because I think that on a Shabbat morning, Jews should be inspired by Torah, and while I like to think that I am as well read as anyone, at the end of the day, I read the same op-eds that everyone else does. I don't speak on Israeli politics because I think it is very tricky to speak about a secular political entity, the modern State of Israel, in a religious context. It can be done, but not in 12-15 minutes between the Torah service and *Musaf*. I don't speak on Israel because in my time here, I have discovered that of the 1500 families in this community, there are a number to the political right and a number to the political left and the rule book for rabbis says: "In your first two years, try your best not to polarize the community with politics." Finally, I don't speak on Israeli politics because with very few exceptions none of us are Israeli. If you want to have a voice in the democratic state of Israel, then do what Jews have dreamt of doing for thousands of years but could only do in the last 62 years: move there. If you live here, if you have yet to make *aliyah*, then know that the Diaspora must tread very carefully before we start telling Israelis how to run their country.

With all of that said, all the disclaimers out of the way, today we are going to walk on new territory. Not because I am going to preach on Israeli politics, I won't. Rather, because as a community we need to respond to Israel's enemies. Not the first kind of enemies, the *oyvekha*, the *m'khunasim*, the ones who are gathering at Israel's doorstep. We know these enemies. We've heard the calls from Iran to destroy the Zionist entity. We know that Hezbollah has three times as many missiles in southern Lebanon right now as it did before the Second Lebanon war – not only more, but bigger, longer, and more accurate than just a few years ago. We know the ongoing threat of suicide bombers, the continued and unconscionable captivity of Gilad Shalit, now held hostage into a fourth year. The enemies of Israel, *oyvekha*, are assembled. They are active and, sadly, we need not look far to see them.

This morning I want to talk about the second kind of enemy that Rashi spoke of: the *rodfim*. These are the enemies who are conducting a pernicious and stealthy conversation in guile around the world, in political, academic, economic, cultural, and other circles, who are trying to delegitimize, demonize, and isolate Israel in the world community. Under the banner of international law, pro-peace slogans, human rights, or other causes, there is a concerted and insidious effort to distort the history of Israel, to undercut her national aspirations, to exaggerate and misrepresent her misdeeds, and to slander her in what can on occasion devolve into retrograde anti-Semitic libel. On one level, there is nothing new about these efforts. This campaign has ebbed and flowed since long before the notorious 1975 "Zionism is Racism" Resolution at the U.N., through repeated equivalency of Zionism and Apartheid, and ongoing chants of "from the river to the seas Palestine will be Free."

In recent years, these efforts have moved from the fringe to the mainstream. Beginning with the notorious Durban Conference of 2001, and then in a campaign initiated in 2005 by 171 Palestinian NGO's, an international campaign known as BDS (Boycott, Divestment, and Sanctions) has created a framework in which Israel has been the subject of relentless attacks, blamed for everything regardless of the truth. Most of us know full well of the notorious Goldstone report, a report that largely overlooked Israeli efforts to protect human life, whitewashing Hamas who routinely employed non-combatants as human shields. We have heard of the situation in England, how through a quirk in the judicial system, representatives from the Israeli military can be arrested for war crimes. How Tzipi Livni, the head of the Israeli opposition, cancelled a visit to the U.K. for fear of being arrested and the Israeli government has advised senior IDF officers not to visit certain countries where they risk being arrested on charges of alleged war crimes.

These efforts are not a problem only in the U.N. or "over there" in Europe. In the business community, there are concerted efforts for Caterpillar, Motorola, and others to divest from Israel. There is an initiative called "code pink," urging women to boycott Ahava beauty products. Several mainline churches call, time and again, for institutions to divest from Israel. Anti-Israel sentiment is perhaps most ubiquitous on college campuses. UC-Berkeley, UC-Irvine, UC-San Diego – there have been "Israel Apartheid Weeks" on more campuses than we can count. On the athletic front, divestment action led to the Davis tennis matches being played behind closed doors with no fans. Just this past week, all of us have read how Elvis Costello cancelled his planned concert to Israel for fear that playing Israel would link him to Israeli oppression. A man who could have used his music, in the way Paul Simon did, to bring people together, has uncourageously fallen victim to the BDS movement. The list goes on and on.

The problem is not that people can't and shouldn't protest Israel. I shop where I want to shop and I make ideological choices all the time where I spend and don't spend my money. I don't begrudge the right of people, even those with whom I vehemently disagree, to make similar decisions. And the problem is not that Israel is perfect. She is not and if you have spent a few minutes with me, you know that my politics are such that I think an open airing of the issues is always a good thing.

The problem with BDS is that between their intimidation and distortions and our own temerity, we have woken up to a world where the people who tell the story of the Middle East most loudly, most forcefully, are not us but our enemies. Diaspora Jewry has lost its way; we have lost our voice when it comes to Israel. We are so shaped by our universalism, by our oozing empathy, that we have somehow come to believe that liberalism and Zionism are at odds with each other. We live in a world where the right of the Israeli Ambassador to speak at Brandeis University has become a question for discussion. In our hesitation, the playing field has been ceded either to the BDS movement, or to those who may not represent our voice. The liberal pro-Israel community has lost its political gumption. We have lost our ability to make positive statements about Israel, both convinced and convincing, respectful of the counterclaims of others, but unflinching in the strength of our own beliefs.

I don't care if you are on the political right or left. You are all welcome here at Park Avenue Synagogue. People can debate whether American Jewry should or shouldn't have a voice in the internal affairs of the State of Israel. What I care about, what I feel a responsibility for, is the tone and content of the Israel conversation here, in the Diaspora, where all of us live. I feel passionately that we educate our children and adults with a knowledge, love for, and contact with Israel so they can respond with their own voice to what is being said about the Jewish homeland. I would love nothing more than for our community to be a place of vibrant debate, where people speak from the left, from the right, even from the center. Would it be, when it comes to Israel, that everyone was a prophet, that we were all worthy of rising to the occasion, to speak about the modern miracle of Israel. I hope that in the next year and years to come, our adult learning, our schools, all reflect a commitment to developing the congregational toolbox to respond to Israel's ideological enemies. What we cannot do is sit on the sidelines as Israel is being delegitimized in the world community. We need to regain our nerve, to have a bit of *chutzpah* when it comes to Israel.

In a few moments we will rise to say the prayer for the state of Israel, as we do every week. I began to think about Elvis Costello, whose music I love, and his decision not to go to Israel. It is his right, his decision, however misguided, if he doesn't want his music associated with Israel. But I have rights too and I also have something else – a pulpit. Frankly, I think there is nothing funny about Boycotts, Divestments, and Sanctions. And I started to think…while I can't change his decision, why grant him the last word? If he won't go to Israel, then I will bring Israel to him. What if, on this quiet three-day weekend, we were to sing the prayer for the state of Israel to his music? What if we adapted the words of the prayer for Israel to his most identifiable song ("Allison")? What if word got out and next weekend a few more congregations sang the prayer for the state of Israel to Elvis Costello's music, and so on and so on? What if, soon enough, we were able to generate a generational Pavlovian response to Elvis Costello whereby singing his music became associated with support for Israel? Now wouldn't that be a *chutzpahdik* way to respond to him? Wouldn't that be a nice way to respect his right to do what he wants and to maintain our right to respond as we wish? Wouldn't that be a nice way to end a sermon, wouldn't that be a great way to begin a much larger movement.

Note: *Cantor Elana Rozenfeld led the congregation in singing the prayer for the state of Israel to the tune of Elvis Costello's "Allison."*

Koraḥ

"Pyramids of Success"

Coach John Wooden passed away in Los Angeles last Friday night, June 4, at the age of 99. Having grown up in the backyard of UCLA, I lived very much in the shadow of this towering college basketball coach affectionately called the "Wizard of Westwood." His ten NCAA Championships at UCLA in a 12-year period stand as an unmatched record. His UCLA teams won a record 88 games in a row, 98 straight home games in Pauley Pavilion, four perfect 30-0 seasons. He was and remains a legend. To say that John Wooden experienced success in his lifetime is, to put it mildly, a vast understatement.

It is thus all the more interesting to learn how Wooden defined success. He was fond of telling the story of how, in his youth, a teacher in Indiana asked the class to write an essay in response to the question: "What is success?" At the time, his answer was what you would expect: fame, fortune, or power. But in the years that followed, Wooden grew older, becoming a teacher, a coach, and a parent. He reformulated his answer based on advice he had received from his father years earlier: "Don't worry about being better than somebody else, but never try ceasing to be the best you can be." Long before the world of management gurus and Power Point displays, Wooden drafted a diagram that he would take with him throughout his career, giving it to all his players – a document called the "Pyramid of Success." The Pyramid outlines the foundational building blocks and process by which a basketball player, a team, any human being can arrive at success: skill, conditioning, team spirit, confidence, self control, poise, all the things that contribute towards the desired end. The most interesting part of the pyramid is the apex, the peak of success according to Wooden: "Success is the peace of mind that is a direct result of the self-satisfaction of knowing you did your best to become the best that you are capable of being."

Wooden achieved more success as a coach than any of his peers, past or future, more than any person can hope for in his or her given field. But for Wooden, reaching the top had nothing to do with winning or losing, or for that matter, with reaching an external goal. Being successful has nothing to do with being the smartest, the fastest, the richest, the most powerful, or the most beautiful. Being successful has nothing to do with the acknowledgement of your peers or the public. Being successful has to do with two critical ingredients – relentless effort and deep self-awareness. Did you do your best to become the best that you are capable of being? It is folksy, but it is foolproof and it is all about hard work and knowing your capabilities. It is a definition that can be judged only by the person who has to live with the judgment – you. Not society, not a teacher, not your boss, not a standardized test, and not a balance sheet – only you know if you did your best to become the best that you are capable of being.

If you want a study in contrasts, if you want to look at the exact opposite of Wooden's metric of success, then you need look no further than the arch-demagogue of our Torah reading – Koraḥ. Koraḥ, who came to Moses with a list of complaints and a series of demands. In the rabbinic mind, the rebellion of Koraḥ and his followers is emblematic of a controversy that is not *l'shem shamayim*, not for the sake of heaven. The rabbis note an oddity in the very way that Koraḥ's complaint is introduced. The text of our *parasha* reads: "And Koraḥ, son of Izhar, son of Levi, along with Datan and Abiram the sons of Eliav and Ohn son of Reuven… took." Rabbinic tradition noted the odd phrasing of this verse, "and Koraḥ took." It is odd in English as well as in the original Hebrew. What exactly did Koraḥ take? The sentence is missing a direct object. One cannot take without taking something. The rabbis respond to their own question by explaining that the syntax of the verse is an insight into Koraḥ's character – he was by definition "a taker."

It wasn't so much what he said, how he said it, or what he asked for that was the crux of the issue. The problem was that Koraḥ had a corrosive sense of entitlement; he wanted success by way of shortcuts.

He sought recognition and reputation, but not by means of his own efforts. The world owed him and he was going to take, he was going to get his due. But what he thought was his due was a due that was undeserved and could never be satiated. Not once, but twice Moses responds with the rhetorical refrain "Is it not enough for you?" "Is it not enough for you that God made you a distinct people?! Is it not enough for you that God has brought you to a land flowing with milk and honey?!" The word *dayenu* was not in Koraḥ's vocabulary, nor was the idea of being satisfied by means of hard work. In a sense, neither Moses nor God could address his demand, for his very nature would ensure that success would remain forever elusive.

Koraḥ's ambition lacked the two ingredients of Wooden's definition of success – self awareness and hard work. There was nothing inside, no foundation, no cornerstone, nothing to back up his hollow demands. He was someone who wanted a title, recognition, and reputation, but not to earn or deserve them by merit, hard work, or character. There was a disturbing asymmetry between what he wanted and the effort he was willing to put forth.

Success for Wooden, and for all of us, is when there is a consistency between appearances and essence, between effort and expectation. Wooden's pyramid of success is worthy of examination not because he eschews achievement – I am sure Wooden was very proud of his team's winning record – but rather because his ethic insists that success come by way of diligence, knowing oneself, and sustained dedication. Koraḥ had the equation backward.

Public recognition and achievement are not unimportant, on the contrary, they are. All of us need be aware of how our world does and doesn't assign recognition and define success. It would be foolish to think otherwise. But this awareness cannot and should not be determinative. It is striking to consider how elusive normative definitions of success are for all of our Biblical heroes. Think about it. Adam and Eve are thrown out of the Garden of Eden. Sarah, Rebecca, Rachel all die with unfinished business. Jacob and Joseph die in the land of Egypt. Moses never reaches the Promised Land. King David dies loveless and never builds the Temple he was supposed to establish. None of our major Biblical figures get everything done, none of their bucket lists are fully checked off. Yet, these are our matriarchs and patriarchs, our heroes, because in their time, they were the ones who left it all out on the field – they were the ones who achieved success.

So too in our own day, so too in our own lives. My workplace is right here – your synagogue. I look back on the year gone by and I am very proud of what we have done. I also know as we head into summer, that for all our accomplishments, there have also been many mistakes, programs that didn't go the way we hoped, some that never even got off the ground. But I say to myself, and more importantly, say to the professional and lay leadership of the congregation, as long as we know deep down in our heart of hearts that we left it all out on the field, that we worked hard and smart and creatively to the best of our ability, fine – *dayenu*. As Churchill wrote: "Success is never final, failure is never fatal. It's courage that counts." In this season of end-of-year reports, graduation speeches, and other summations, let's make sure that we are judging our community by the metric that we would each ask for ourselves.

It would be nice to think we live in a meritocracy where hard work was always acknowledged, where the industrious were rewarded and the undeserving got what they should get. But we don't live in that world. Sometimes, the wrong person gets the job, the account goes elsewhere, and our best efforts are overlooked by those who are in the position to put us on teams or give us promotions. Sometimes we all are left to squirm in an unfair world. I guarantee that no matter who you are, there will always be someone with a bigger car, a higher GPA, better sermons, or what appears to be a happier home life. Given that this is the case, it seems to me that none of us is well served by letting someone else measure our worth. The best we can do is… our best. The only person who knows whether you delivered everything you are capable of is you. "Success is not," Wooden wrote, "something that others can give to you." It must come from within, from within each of us.

Growing up, I would try to memorize famous quotations, a quirky habit for a kid, but what can you do? I'm not sure how it happened, but clearly Wooden's definition of success made the cut. Since then, I, like many in this room, have experienced a few setbacks and thankfully also enjoyed much for which I am deeply grateful. What

I have come to know, as we all do, is that there are times when we are recipients of misplaced criticism and times when we are granted undeserving praise. This is why I remain grateful for John Wooden's definition of success. Only I know if I gave it my all, only I know if I was true to my ideals, only I know if I did everything to become the best that I am capable of becoming. It is the best, the most difficult, and the most honest measure by which to measure our deeds. Or as Emerson wrote: "Nothing can bring you peace of mind but yourself. Nothing can bring you peace but the triumph of principles."

Park Avenue Synagogue

The Park Avenue Synagogue—Agudat Yesharim (the Association of the Righteous) was founded in 1882. From modest beginnings, it has grown into the flagship congregation of the Conservative Movement.

In 1882 a group of German-speaking Jews founded a synagogue and named it Temple Gates of Hope. A church building at 115 East 86th Street was converted into a synagogue and soon the new congregation was known as the Eighty-Sixth Street Temple. Some twelve years after its founding, the synagogue joined together with Congregation Agudat Yesharim, which was to be the Hebrew name of the congregation, and which appears on the cornerstone of the Rita and George M. Shapiro House at the corner of Madison Avenue and 87th Street. The sermons in this congregation were still preached in German. Later amalgamations were to come. A nearby synagogue, the Seventy-Second Street Temple, itself a product of the earlier merger of Beth Israel and Bikkur Cholim, two congregations that had their beginnings on the Lower East Side in the 1840s and had moved uptown to Lexington Avenue and 72nd Street in 1920, merged with the Eighty-Sixth Street Temple—Agudat Yesharim.

In 1923 the Eighty-Sixth Street Temple petitioned the State of New York to have its name changed to Park Avenue Synagogue, and three years later a new sanctuary was constructed on 87th Street and dedicated in March 1927. This building remains the present-day sanctuary. In 1928 the last of the mergers took place when Atereth Israel, a congregation of Alsatian Jews who worshipped in their building on East 82nd Street, added their strength to the Park Avenue Synagogue.

Designed by architect Walter Schneider in 1926, the synagogue building is Moorish in architecture and is one of the last synagogues to have been built in this style, which first became popular in the 1850s in Europe. It features one of the most beautiful cast stone façades in New York and a hand-painted *Bimah*. Moorish decoration is used throughout the interior of the sanctuary, from Arabesque dadoes to the design for the domed ceiling.

In 1954 a new building was dedicated in memory of Rabbi Milton Steinberg, who had come to the Park Avenue Synagogue in 1933. It was designed by Kelly and Gruzen with architect Robert Greenstein (a Park Avenue Synagogue congregant and former student of Le Corbusier). The renowned American artist Adolph Gottlieb was commissioned to design its stained glass curtain wall façade, the largest continuous expanse of stained glass of its time. Gottlieb's images were intended to reflect Rabbi Steinberg's teachings, which advocated the integration of traditional Jewish practice within modernity and American experience.

In 1980 this building was incorporated into the Rita and George M. Shapiro House, housing the educational facilities of the synagogue. It features a distinctive rusticated façade of Mankato limestone, the color of Jerusalem stone when fully matured, and was designed by Bassuk Panero & Zelnick architects and modified by Schuman, Lichenstein, Calman & Efron with the assistance of James Rush Jarrett and Dean Bernard Spring of the School of Architecture at City University.

Prominently displayed on its façade are two bronze sculptures by Nathan Rapoport, "Tragedy and Triumph." The lower bas relief depicts Dr. Janusz Korczak surrounded by the children of his orphanage in Warsaw as they were deported to their death at Treblinka. The upper panel depicts three Israelis – a pioneer, a soldier, and an older man—carrying back to Israel the *Menorah* that was removed from the Temple by Titus and the Romans during Jerusalem's destruction. The inscribed dedication reads: "To the sacred memory of the million Jewish children who perished in the Holocaust." Above the dedication is the Hebrew word *Zakhor* – Remember. Dedicated as a living memorial to the Holocaust, this building expresses Park Avenue Synagogue's hope that the memory of these children will inspire new generations of educated and proud Jews and ensure the continuity of Jewish tradition, history, faith, and heritage.

Park Avenue Synagogue Board of Trustees, Clergy, and Staff

Officers
Steven M. Friedman, *Chairman*
Brian G. Lustbader, *President*
Marcia Eppler Colvin, *Vice President*
Paul M. Corwin, *Vice President*
Howard Rubin, *Vice President*
Arthur Penn, *Treasurer*
Marlene Muskin, *Associate Treasurer*
Rachael First, *Secretary*

Honorary Chairmen
Amy A.B. Bressman
Joel J. Cohen
Geoffrey J. Colvin
Alan Levine
Martin J. Milston
Nathaniel H. Usdan

Honorary Presidents
Robert P. Antler
Arthur H. Bienenstock
Menachem Z. Rosensaft
Paul S. Schreiber

Honorary Vice Presidents
Joanne V. Davis
Bernard Goldberg
Leon I. Heller
David Parker
A. Stanley Robinson
Arnold L. Sabin

Clergy and Staff
Elliot J. Cosgrove, Ph.D., *Rabbi*
Steven I. Rein, *Assistant Rabbi*
David H. Lincoln, *Rabbi Emeritus*
Nancy Abramson, *Cantor*
Elana Rozenfeld, *Cantor*
Azi Schwartz, *Cantor*
David Lefkowitz, *Cantor Emeritus*
Beryl P. Chernov, *Executive Director*
Neil Zuckerman, *Director of Congregational Education*
Julia Andelman, *Director of Adult Education and Community Programs*
Ron Koas, *Director, Congregational School*
Carol Hendin, *Director, Early Childhood Center*
Jason Oppenheimer, *Director of Youth Activities and Rabbi Judah Nadich High School*
Matthew Check, *Director of Young Family Education*
Marga Hirsch, *Director, Edmond de Rothschild Library and PAS Bulletin Editor*
John Davis, *Facilities Director*
Lawrence Conley, *Director of Media*

Honorary Trustees
Leslie Agisim
Lucy Becker
Barry Bryer
Nadine Habousha Cohen
Andrew Fier
Katherina Grunfeld
Martin Halbfinger
Laurie Harris
Ellen Harrow
Joel Hirschtritt
Amos Kaminski
Bea Kaplan
Gershon Kekst
Millard Midonick
Morris M. Podolsky
Joann Abrams Rosoff
Shereen Rutman
Joan Schefler
David Sekons
Lawrence Soicher
Ray Treiger
Adam Usdan

Board Of Trustees
Natalie Barth
Daniel Bernstein
Darcy Dalton
James Druckman
Susan Edelstein
Michael Fruchtman
Henry Glanternik
Richard Green
Lynn Halbfinger
Nancy Hirschtritt
Andrew Hoine
Floy Kaminski
Dennis Karr
Isaac Lemor
Ivan Lustig
Freema Nagler
Judith Poss
Alain Roizen
Willa Rosenberg
Jean Bloch Rosensaft
Suzette Rubinstein
Joan Schreiber
Melvin Schweitzer
Heidi Silverstone
Wendy Slavin
Karen Smul
Jonathan Sobel
Marcia Stone
Barbara Weinstein

Advisory Council
James Aisenberg
Robert Becker
Jena Berlinski
Jason Dolinsky
Jennifer Feldman
Edward Fisher
Jeffrey Flug
Anita Gluck
Mark Goodman
Fred Kastenbaum
Stephanie Leichter
Rochelle Ludwig
Andrea Lustig
Steven Mandelsberg
Jaya Nahmiyas
Rise Norman
James Rosenfeld
Erica Schultz
Caryn Seidman Becker
Annette Sherman
Diane Smallberg
Dawn Spiera
Aaron Stern
Mark Wasserberger
Meryl Wiener

Arms
Evelyn Gelman, *Women's Evening Group*
Susan Lerner, *Women's Evening Group*
Sherry Cohen, *Sisterhood*
Jason Dolinsky, *Men's Club*
Jessie Harris, *Young Couples Group*
Tamara Stark, *Young Couples Group*
Leslie Agisim, *Singles*
Jennifer Hoine, *Early Chilhood Center Parents' Association*
Stephanie Leichter, *Early Chilhood Center Parents' Association*
Erica Friedman, *Congregational School Parents' Association*
Pamela Hirsch, *Congregational School Parents' Association*
Elizabeth Lewis, *Congregational School Parents' Association*